S0-AYV-157

Buhari

A Family Odyssey in Nepal

Linda Schuyler Horning

To Samyukta
For Sarita
Namaste!

Copyright © 2017 Linda Schuyler Horning

All rights reserved. Copying or reproducing any part of this work without prior written permission from the copyright holder is a violation of federal copyright law.

Sasu Aama Books

All rights reserved.

ISBN: 0-9991087-0-0

ISBN-13: 978-0-9991087-0-3

Sasu Aama Books is a Nepal-inspired brand related to parenting and inspirational memoir.

This book is a work of creative nonfiction. It reflects the author's recollection of experiences, though some events may not be entirely factual. Names have been changed to protect the privacy of individuals, some events have been altered or compressed, and some dialogue has been recreated.

COVER DESIGN AND ILLUSTRATION
BY ROBIN HART

COPY EDITING
BY POLLY ZETTERBERG

To my family

Linda Schuyler Horning

CONTENTS

ACKNOWLEDGMENTS

I will always feel gratitude toward those who helped me bring this book to fruition. First, without my family, there would be no story to tell. They made an incredible memory with me, which I felt compelled to write down.

The wonderful people I came to know at Sierra Writers, whether as members, guest speakers, or part of my critique group, provided needed expertise and shared their experiences with me. To those who read, supported and offered comments, I am eternally grateful. Others served as mentors, often without meaning to do so. Finally, thanks to those who allowed me to quote their remarks, and completed the editing and design. I could not have finished this project without you.

"Do not dwell in the past, do not dream of the future, concentrate the mind on the present moment". -- Buddha

PROLOGUE

In 2007, my husband, Paul, and I saved three weeks for travel, making possible a trek in Nepal with our son. We chose November that first time because it's the favored season, after the summer monsoons and before the weather turns very cold. Adam met us at the Kathmandu airport alone.

I was ready to see a thinner frame because Adam had told me via email messages he'd been sick, warning of a waning physique. But the emaciated man that stood waving to us from outside the crowd-control gate was hardly recognizable as my son. His hollow cheeks and sunken eye sockets reminded me of pictures I'd seen of World War II concentration camps; I was shocked and in disbelief, and the cab ride soon to follow compounded my concern. Adam asked the driver to stop so he could lean out his side door to throw up.

It took two days of searching in Kathmandu to find a clinic staffed with Western doctors equipped to provide a new diagnosis and get Adam's health condition turned around. They prescribed long-term antibiotics which arrested his weight loss and enabled normal bowel absorption; weight gain became possible again. We learned tropical sprue was the culprit, not a parasite as his local doctor had suspected before. Recovery began for Adam almost overnight, and as Paul and I fed him high calorie foods, we all felt better again.

"I appreciate you guys being here for me. It matters more than I thought it would," Adam quietly told us. I remember that admission as the first of many miracles I would witness that year in Nepal.

Adam lived in Pokhara then, so we returned with him to hike short distances in the mountains that surround the town. Mount Sarankot and the World Peace Pagoda, both demanding climbs in themselves, offered an opportunity to test our fitness and make sure Adam was strong enough before any of us tried to do more. As we grew stronger, hiking the west side of the Annapurna Circuit began to seem doable in the time we had left. All three of us finished that trek in the ten days that followed without suffering so much as a blister on our feet. Considering how unfit we all were at the start, that outcome ranks in my mind as miracle number two.

Even though Adam gained seven pounds while hiking five hours a day, we brought him home to the United States at the end of the trek to recuperate with us. After a six-month stay, he regained the rest of his weight, and without hesitation, decided Nepal was where he wanted to be. He bid us good-bye once again and traveled back the way he had come.

Before our arrival in Nepal this time (2014), Paul and I took a two-day stopover in Hong Kong. While checking messages that first evening, I read Adam's posting on Facebook saying he and Amita got married. The news left me crestfallen. I wanted us to be with them at this special time. The post had dozens of "likes", but none of them were mine.

Feeling left out of my son's life is foreign to me. We'd bonded well from day one, and no other babies came along to steal my attention from him. I tried to let him go, to let him live his life as a man, but memories keep flooding back to me, of the baby and child who needed his mother, and later the mother who needed him.

Our family lived in a lot of places when Adam was young. Born in San Diego, he moved with us to Australia just after turning one. For over two years, he saw Santa Claus in summer and played with wallabies in the campground. When we returned to the States, we took a longer route, enabling Adam to literally circle the globe before starting school.

Reflecting on his life this way, I should have known Adam would want to travel on his own when he came of age, but one other factor played an even larger role in his desire to live overseas. Paul's time in the Peace Corps had led to extensive traveling before we met, exposing young Adam to stories of life in Iran before the revolution, and Afghanistan before war in the Middle East. Paul waxed nostalgic about countries foreign to most people in the United States, and instilled in Adam values antithetical to those that treat immigrants and foreigners as inferior to ourselves.

At San Francisco State, Adam's choice of a dual major in International Relations and Political Science fit right into the script. Visiting Nepal even before graduating, Adam immediately began talking about living overseas. Only then did I realize my sense of loss and what such a move by him would mean to me.

Part 1

KATHMANDU

CULTURAL CHALLENGES IN THE CITY

Chapter One

Welcome to Nepal

It is April of 2014. Our flight into Tribhuvan International Airport arrives about an hour late, enveloping us in darkness before Paul and I get the view of the Kathmandu Valley we crave. Ringed by snow-covered peaks, Nepal sits northeast of India, in the middle of the Himalayan mountain range. A landlocked country, Nepal contains Mount Everest, the tallest mountain in the world.

Ancient temples and modest dwellings fill this hidden land, with few roads to connect them. Not until the year I was born, 1949, did the first motorized vehicles appear. Then, whole limousines were carried over the mountains secured to long bamboo poles. They arrived as most goods did, strapped to the shoulders of porters. In 1956, a road was built linking Kathmandu to the Indian border, which accelerated trade from outside.

Tourism is Nepal's largest industry. Paul and I arrive for a second trip, not merely as tourists, but as parents visiting a son. This country has been Adam's home for the last eight years; he arrived here first to witness the political struggle, then

15

stayed on to work in human rights. He's proud of his achievements, as are we, although they've come with a price. His commitment to living overseas has meant long separations from us, and the risk of losing touch with an extended family back in the States.

We find the airport barely changed in seven years; still void of expensive embellishments common to more prosperous nations. Walls of bare concrete and brick shelter shopkeepers selling miniature prayer wheels and Tibetan singing bowls. We stand with others in long lines of exhausted travelers while customs and visa officials process our papers. Our bags wait for us as we enter the claim area; local time is nearing midnight before we clear the final gate.

Kathmandu air and noise assault us as we step out the door. Cab drivers shout "taxi" and trip over each other to be first to reach us and earn our business. The night air is suffused with the dust of so many unpaved roads. It is springtime and the end of the dry season. The monsoons are coming, but we're hoping they'll hold off long enough for us to finish another trek. Looking for our son, we know he'll be here to meet us. Over the heads of shorter, darker natives, we see him waving.

This time, Adam stands strong and handsome, and towers protectively over his new wife, Amita. They make a nice-looking couple, if you don't notice the difference in their heights. Adam, at six feet, dwarfs his Nepali wife, who stands a full foot shorter. Yet I'm comforted in knowing someone else now keeps an eye on my son.

Tears don't well up when I see him. I hadn't wanted them to. Since I'm meeting his wife for the first time, I want my first impression to be strong. Hugging my son, I bravely hold my emotions in check.

Paul's hug ends in a handshake, as it often does when he greets his son. His aviation-style eyeglasses enhance a stern expression, then it falls away, melting into a warm smile. Still blond, but darkening, his full head of hair makes him look younger than most men of his age. He greets Amita with a friendly confidence drawn from years of living abroad.

Amita speaks softly, "Welcome to Nepal," and lays a white silk scarf, called a *khata,* around each of our necks. Her smile stretches across a flawless caramel-colored face encompassing two sparkling brown Asian eyes. Her natural warmth casts any fears I had about meeting her off onto the evening breeze.

The driver Adam hired stuffs our two suitcases into the rear of his tiny Suzuki Maruti. Not a true luggage compartment, the shallow space in the back allows no more than a foot of storage. I remembered to protect my laptop with extra padding, but hold my breath until the liftgate finally clicks into place. The driver comes around to open the rear door for us, gesturing to indicate where we should sit.

Three of us squeeze into the back seat holding our backpacks on our laps. Six-foot Adam is wedged against the far door. Amita sits in the middle, with me on her other side, while Paul sits in the front passenger seat.

Just as we think this tight arrangement might work, I watch as a new passenger attempts to climb into the back seat with my son. Adam pushes back, firmly saying, "*Ka'ĩ khaali chaina!*" "There is no room for you in here!"

His protest fails to discourage the extra passenger, who diverts to the front seat where he perches next to the driver, a willing accomplice in this. With the stick shift held firmly between his knees, he and the driver get the car into gear and commence driving us down the bumpy street.

Now Adam says, "We'd be a lot safer with less of a crowd in the front." He turns to his wife, urging her best Nepali diatribe.

"*Ekaichin yãã kaar thaamnuparchaand!*" she pleads. "Please stop the car!" She asks the extra passenger to climb into the back seat with us.

All is to no avail. By now, both the driver and his friend are satisfied; the driver has succeeded in providing free transportation for his friend, as was his original intent.

Conceding defeat, Adam quietly leans forward to instruct his father, "*Bistaarai hããknuholaa*' means 'Please drive more slowly' and '*Hos garnu*' means 'Be careful'. They're two phrases you might find useful here."

My white-knuckled grip on the handle above my side window chooses now to loosen completely, the handle coming off into my hand. Showing it to Adam, a nervous giggle escapes from my throat.

"Welcome to Nepal," he says, smiling.

I shrug, releasing the tension I'd felt.

"Thanks," I say. "I'd forgotten. This is all part of

the Nepali experience. I should relax and go with it, or I'll be wasting my time."

Our taxi ride from the airport ends in a gated parking lot, where even at this late hour, a middle-aged porter waits up for us. He wears the traditional Nepali cloth cap, or *topi*, and a matching brown and white tunic top, and chats affably in English as he leads us through the entrance and helps us carry our bags up the stairs. A one-bedroom apartment, owned by Adam's friend, Bibek, waits for us at the rear of this bank building. We climb broad marble steps and follow a polished wooden banister to the third floor, where the hallways are covered with plastic drop cloths and the smell of fresh latex paint hangs in the air.

"Bibek told me it would be ready," says Adam, clearly disappointed in his friend. "Look at how much there still is to do." He wears a grim expression as he shoves our key into the lock, but his face brightens as he steps inside the room.

Glistening white, with a 30-inch LCD television screen hanging on one wall, our room looks modern and clean, and, as an added bonus, a small kitchenette stands off to one side, providing access to a sink, two gas burners, and an upright refrigerator/freezer. Since we're paying only US$150 per week to stay here, we see the bargain in this.

"You just don't see places like this in Nepal." says Adam. "Well, at least not for this price."

Spreading her arms wide and twirling, Amita agrees. "Look at this place, Adam! Bibek had it ready for us, just as he said he would."

Adam and Amita sit down with us on matching

settee and chairs. Paul and I are eager to spend time with them in spite of the late hour. Our sleep cycles are so messed up at this point that day and night feel much the same.

"I didn't understand why you made that comment on Facebook about Amita and I getting married without waiting for you." I'd shared my hurt feelings with another Facebook friend, while forgetting Adam had access to the same thread. "I want you to know that was only the paperwork, and we're planning a real wedding celebration in Pokhara that you're both invited to attend."

"I just figured we'd have a meal or two together before we go on the trek," I say. "Do you have something else planned?"

"Well, yea-ah," he says, with emphasis on the 'yea-ah.' "Amita's aunt is setting up a Hindu wedding ceremony at a temple complex there. You and Dad will be part of it."

"That could be fun," I say, a bit hesitant. "What will we wear? We didn't bring any dress clothes, and I don't think we want to wear our hiking pants." Then, warming to the idea, I remember a photo of Amita wearing a beautiful red *sari*. I'd shared it on Facebook with everyone I know.

"I could buy a sari!" I declare, excitement growing inside me.

"Now wait," Adam says. "Amita and I have talked about that. We've decided you'd be better off having a *kurta* made. Saris are hard to wear, and they're always coming loose. Amita wears safety pins everywhere to hold hers in place. A kurta is a better choice. They're way more practical."

Cocking my head to one side, I listen carefully while Amita describes the kurta in more detail. She says it's like a tunic or dress with loose pajama pants or tights worn underneath. A long matching scarf drapes around the neck and may be worn over the head to cover the wearer's hair.

"You see them all the time on the street," she says, "but they can be very beautiful if made of the right fabric and colors."

"I'm sold," I say, "but the first thing I want to look for is an unlocked cell phone."

Talking about kurtas and cell phones in the same breath seems a bit surreal, but I'd told Adam before we left that buying a new phone is high on my list. I know my regular cell phone won't work in Nepal, and I don't want to buy a new one without first making sure it can be used in countries outside the United States.

"Amita can help you with that tomorrow," he says. "We'll both come over and have lunch together. Then Amita can take you shopping while I go to an internet cafe and catch up on some work."

It becomes clear that Amita will be our guide while Adam continues to work through the end of the week. He had proposed a timeline while we were still in California that keeps us in Kathmandu while he finishes his work schedule, then he'll join us full-time once we leave town to start on our trek. We haven't decided yet just which trek we want to take, but I'm beginning to suspect it will be somewhere near Pokhara, since the wedding celebration will take place there first.

Chapter Two

HOLD MY HAND

Three uniformed bank guards stand and bow to us as Paul and I prepare to go through the horizontal sliding gate about 7 a.m. Our apartment location makes it very secure.

"Namaste," we say, pressing our palms together.

"Namaste" return the men with big smiles. They seem pleased to be addressed in this way.

Turning back to Paul, I say, "I could get used to this. They make me feel as if we've got our own private honor guard."

Outside the gate, a short, paved alleyway runs parallel to the bank building, ending where a concrete sidewalk, alongside the four-lane boulevard, accommodates several buses. Noise intensifies as we approach the traffic, which divided in the middle by a low metal fence.

Paul and I are just coming up to the sidewalk when I'm stopped by a man in matted braids carrying a basket of Hindu offerings. As I turn, he deftly applies a spot of vermilion to my forehead, leaving me startled and confused about what I should do next. His other hand stretches out before me, making his meaning clear. Since I have no rupees, I simply shrug and mime my lack, but the incident amps up our urgency to find a money changer before more issues like this arise.

Thamel is a renowned shopping district which lies conveniently in an area just across the boulevard from our apartment. While the traffic is light at this early hour, and crossing the boulevard will be easier, we've no stop lights to help us, and traffic laws, as we know them in America, are not the same.

Still tentative, we prepare to cross where white cross-hatchings on the pavement indicate it might be safe. Paul takes my hand and we wait. Other pedestrians, obviously more practiced at this, gather to our left and right. In front stands a young woman with long black hair, wearing a peach-colored tunic and matching scarf. With Amita's kurta description fresh in my mind, the street becomes a fashion runway, and my fellow pedestrians are models of various ages and styles.

The first break in traffic comes in front of a group of three slower motorcycles. We cross to the median, along with a family of four. All wear some sort of tunic top with loose-fitting pants, but the women wear coordinating colors, while the men prefer brown and black. While I study their clothing, two buses to our left stop traffic to let off passengers, and we stroll to the other side.

As we enter the ancient dirt alleyway, dust rises with my every step. Sidewalks are rare in Thamel.

The low-cut hikers I wear do a decent job of protecting my feet, but I wonder how the women around me manage to keep their bright-colored sandals so clean. If it were me wearing the sandals, they'd be ruined by the end of the day.

Dust can also be a problem for the many shops and businesses in Thamel. Since most open onto an unpaved alley, clothing and wares prominently displayed in doorways need constant attention to keep them looking like new. We hear the sound of multiple metal security doors rolling open as shops begin to set up their businesses for the day.

At a shop about halfway down one alley, a clean-shaven young man sits at a window facing the street. He takes our American dollars and counts out Nepali rupees in exchange.

"One hundred rupees equals almost a full American dollar," he explains. "Calculations will be very easy for you to do. If you pay 200 rupees for something, it will be the same as paying about two American dollars. The decimal point, moved two places to the left, will be your conversion guide."

Breakfast is in the open-air dining room of a small hotel. Stepping directly off the unpaved street, we find ourselves on the floor of a dining room. The tables are filled with diners of all ages and nationalities, creating a rhythm of multilingual accents and tones.

I revel in the mixture of people, tuning into their conversations despite competition from noise on the street. Glancing around at the other tables, I pay little attention to the solicitous waiter who asks for my order.

"Scrambled eggs and oat porridge (*porri*)," I say. Then, as an after-thought, '*dudh chia*'—milk tea. My mouth waters in anticipation. Each waft of cooking odors from the kitchen increases my appetite for new flavors and textures awaiting me.

As it turns out, my meal is just okay, and Paul's eggs-over-easy are overdone, but with only 325 rupees on our bill, we can afford to make a few mistakes. Judging from the food we see on the plates of others, our skill in ordering needs a serious update.

Foremost on our minds, as we rush back to our apartment, is a chance to take a long shower before Adam and Amita arrive. Soon we'll be out on the trail, with modern bathroom facilities, like the ones we have in the United States, unavailable to us anywhere.

At 10 a.m., Amita sweeps into the room dressed in shorts and a sleeveless top, stylishly set off with a navy blue and white scarf and perky straw hat. Adam follows in blue jeans and a black t-shirt. They help Paul and me with some housekeeping issues: a missing waste bin and a barely functioning shower drain. Bibek promises to deal with them before we return from our excursion into Thamel.

After a quick lunch together, Adam finds his internet cafe where he will do some work while Amita stays with us. I appreciate her willingness to spend time with us when we've only just met, but, as I'm soon to discover, she will show us more than a simple courtesy. As the day unfolds, Amita reveals how she views our family from her own cultural perspective.

Amita firmly takes my hand, and then simply won't let it go. At first her hand-holding just makes me feel safer in the heavy traffic, but she has another purpose in mind. As she steers me this way and that, ducking into doorways and dashing between cars, she presents a picture to others on the street. Among the brightly colored tunics and matching scarves of traditionally dressed women, here is Amita, obviously Nepali, but not dressed as one, and with her, these two older white people cling to her. We are so obviously not from here.

In the eyes of Nepali society, the mother-in-law owns a higher status in the family. As we enter the city, bystanders watch Amita closely, wondering about my relationship to her. Their stares, frowns, or smiles seem to indicate where we fit in. In her country, Amita has a role to play, apparent to us from that very first time we crossed the street.

Paul has no choice but to fall behind, but I can tell from his smile that he likes this new development and finds amusement in what's going on. He keeps pace with us, watching every nuanced expression from the rear. This is just another cultural experience for him, among many he's shared around the world.

Amita smiles broadly, as well. Even as I change positions, she grabs an elbow and marches on. Our hands get clammy as they will in the noonday heat, but this presents no deterrent to her. It's obvious we are not tourists, and she only a guide. With the hand-holding, we are somehow related, and I am most likely her mother-in-law.

I feel pale next to Amita, but pale is good in Nepal. Many, including Amita, use cosmetic products to purposely lighten their skin. Dark skin is associated with the common laborer, and is not thought to be beautiful. Most Nepali women see it as a flaw, yet I walk among these ageless Asian beauties feeling somewhat embarrassed by my white wrinkled skin.

Not so for Amita. She holds her head high, showing no discomfort at the spectacle we present. The ancient dirt alleyways are home to many older, more traditional Nepali women and men. More accustomed to putting on a dour expression and downward glance at Amita's bare knees, they now look up and smile at the company she keeps. My whiteness confers a certain status to her.

True to her word, Amita delivers us to a shop on the far side of Thamel, where we find a dealer of cell phones, but I don't have a clue which one I want to buy. Paul is no help. Electronics never were his forte. He immediately starts nodding off where he sits on a stool next to the counter in this open-walled store.

Most American women in their late twenties would have felt frustrated by now, but Amita isn't like any young women I know. Even though she's been saddled with these two older people who can't seem to make up their minds, she remains undeterred. Pulling out her own cell phone, she calls Adam for advice about which one we should buy.

Despite his help, we are unable make a decision. The jet lag has taken its toll, leaving both Paul and I exhausted and longing to park ourselves somewhere, anywhere we can get some sleep. Shaking Paul gently, I get him to his feet, asking Amita to kindly return us to our apartment.

If Amita is frustrated by our lack of decision-making, she doesn't show it. Leaving behind a feeling of warmth and kinship, she hugs us at the door. She'll return with Adam later this same afternoon. They plan to take us to a trekking outfitter back in Thamel.

The idea of another excursion does not appeal. "Don't wake me if I'm still asleep when they come back," I tell Paul, collapsing exhausted beside him on the bed. "I want to seem at least a little coherent when we go out later tonight."

As I drift off to sleep, my thoughts are of Amita and what a loving person she seems to be. On the outside, she projects an image of a modern Western woman, while on the inside she's as traditionally Nepali as they come. How, I wonder, is she going to manage this blending of cultures as she lives her life with my son?

Chapter Three

NOCTURNAL EPIPHANY

I awaken to voices and a door closing as Paul returns from his shopping trip with Adam and Amita. My afternoon nap leaves me refreshed, my jet lag diminished, but not overcome. It still lurks in the shadows, ready to sap my energy and cloud my judgement. I dress hurriedly, catching up on what I missed while the rest of the party moved on.

We'll dine at one of Adam's favorite haunts, where one can order a hookah of smoldering apple-flavored tobacco along with an appetizer and entrée. A pleasant fifteen-minute stroll takes us back into the dusty streets of Thamel.

Three hundred rupees gets me a glass of burgundy and a mellower mood, enabling me to absorb our surroundings from a perch on the second-floor balcony. We look out over a busy mix of pedestrians, bicycles, and street vendors. Prayer flags mingle with strings of lights and billboards, all competing for equal attention. People-watching is acceptable and easy.

Adam and I discuss the merits of cell phones while observing a dark-skinned man in a salmon-colored topi hat and sandals. He solicits patrons for his two-wheeled pedal cab, successfully negotiating a price, then helping an elderly man and his young female companion to clamber inside.

"Would a pedal cab driver use a cell phone to find his way to another part of town?" I ask Adam.

"He would," Adam assures me, "but if this pedal cab driver pulled out a cell phone right now, it would seriously damage my image of him."

"Nepal is so full of charm," I say to Adam. "Nothing is dull or ordinary. I can see why you like it here."

A Rastafari man ambles down the street in dreadlocks and Caribbean pants, arms locked with a woman costumed in a similar fashion, except for her long loose-flowing hair. I envy their youth, their relaxed posture and attitude. Adam and Amita sit across from me displaying similar qualities. Despite the more obvious physical differences, they seem perfectly matched for each other. Adam's long, white arms encircle Amita's bare shoulders with a relaxed intimacy. He's a different son than the one we visited seven years ago. Our former son was uncomfortable around women, and always alone, distant, and impatient much of the time. The new Adam is sure of himself, and more composed. I sit back to enjoy being with them.

Adam looks handsome in the muted light of votive candles decorating our table. With a mother's bias, I examine the facial features most cultures prize. High cheekbones, full lips, large and expressive Germanic blue eyes stare back at me. I find it incomprehensible that love evaded him until he reached age thirty-four.

The hookah is delivered to our table with extra mouthpieces. Adam and Amita get the tobacco burning well, and then pass the pipe's hose across the table with a clean mouthpiece on the end. Paul coughs after his first draw on the pipe, but I manage to hold mine in. The tobacco is smooth and sweet, but soon starves my brain of oxygen and my head begins to spin.

Laughing, I say, "I'm glad there isn't more than just flavored tobacco in that bowl." Then I pass the mouthpiece back across the table to them.

Our first *dal bhat* of the trip doesn't disappoint. We devour the Nepali national dish with gusto, knowing more will be served before we are through. The waiter ladles a second helping of dal into my bowl, but I pass on the steamed rice, taking instead a small mound of curried potatoes, and some spicy *achar*, the colorful chutney-like accent. Accustomed as a local to eating large amounts of rice, Adam nods twice while being served, allowing another large mound to occupy his plate. He finishes all before I do.

Power lines and multi-colored pennant strings form a canopy across the street below. Entwined with them, twinkle lights, indiscernible a moment ago, now sparkle brightly to compound the Eastern mood. Bathed in this ambiance, Nepal has a beguiling appeal, but as the wine and jet lag work their combined effect, a tinge of melancholy begins to overtake me. The undercurrent of discontent with which I battle spoils my enjoyment, and an ominous feeling looms over the evening ahead.

Paul and I soon part from Adam and Amita and head back to our apartment. We're beyond exhausted. Two flights of stairs up to our apartment are like mountains, and the bed a distant peak. Slumber comes quickly as our weary bodies hit the mattress and we nestle into our pillows.

I awake to a light coming from the bathroom. This confuses me and I think morning has come too soon, only to realize Paul has turned on the light, and it's only 2 a.m.! At once angry and frustrated, I am aghast that he would wake me when I was so sound asleep. Didn't he know how much I wanted this sleep, needed this sleep, just to feel normal? The anger only serves to increase wakefulness until I'm forced to absorb the sickening reality that a good night's sleep has eluded me again.

Unable to rest once Paul returns to bed, I climb out of bed and start pacing. I am irrational. In a manic state, I stride around the apartment working myself into a frenzy. Now it is more than sleep I have lost, it is my son. I rant aloud, "Why is my only child living in this place? I am losing him, not just to Nepal, but to this new family. I'll soon be too old to come here again. He will leave us forever, and his children will be born in this country, far away from us, without a chance to know us as their grandparents."

The ranting rings in my ears, and regrettably in Paul's, as well, and then I begin to hear it, and know it for what it is. Fear, masquerading as a need to control my life, my son, and his future. I fear not only what is happening now, but that which has yet to happen.

When the release comes, it comes in a torrent. I am at once ashamed and grief-stricken by my selfish attitude and my lack of control. Where is the love I have for my son? Where is the acceptance? The realization hits me with such force that I break into sobs, each sob lowering me slowly back from whence it came.

In bed now, Paul rubs my back. The sobs continue, but more slowly. I don't deserve the consolation. I am unhappy with the person I am right now. This fear, I begin to realize, has been holding me back, and keeping me from fully enjoying the gift I've been given. I'm visiting my son in this beautiful place, and meeting his sweet new wife. I'm asked to participate in a special ceremony, and all I can think about is what I will lose. I'm being given so much more.

Live in the moment, I tell myself. *Love what I have now, and let go of what I only imagine.* The positive thoughts calm me, and I turn inward again. Sighing heavily, I sigh again. Gratitude returns, and then peace.

Paul goes back to sleep, and I focus on thoughts I need to let go. They are myths from my childhood. Not all of them were good, but the one about falling in love and living happily ever after always appealed. Growing up in Pennsylvania, most of the people I knew who got married tended to settle near home and raise their families with aunts, uncles, and grandparents nearby.

That hadn't happened for my parents, nor did it happen for me. My siblings lived near my home, but I moved to California right after marrying. My mother was present at Adam's birth, but Dad had already passed. Adam grew up without knowing any relatives very well. They were just too far away. I had wanted closer family relationships for my son, but things didn't turn out that way.

When we wake again, Paul and I decide we need to pay more attention to our health. It's obvious we won't get over our jet lag if we keep up the current pace. We send Adam an email message telling him we're taking the day off and will come to his apartment later in the day. He has no problem with our decision, sending the directions we'll need for our cab ride. They seem relieved at the added break our change of plans gives to them. After all, this will be the first time they'll entertain us in their home.

Chapter Four

LALITPUR

A ride to Lalitpur takes about 20 minutes under normal traffic conditions, but today's ride is fraught with bottlenecks, especially when approaching a bridge. I sit quietly, still emotionally drained by my nocturnal outburst, while watching our driver repeatedly lean out his window to speak to other drivers at each traffic stop. Paul and I determine the driver doesn't understand the directions we gave him, so he's asking others for directions to Adam's street.

At the next stop, I hand the driver a small notebook I carry and point to the phone number I'd written down for Amita. "She speaks Nepali," I say, and the driver nods his understanding. He pulls over and dials her number, and she answers on the first ring. A conversation ensues.

Their street is actually an alleyway between buildings. It's bumpy and filled with obstacles such as manhole covers not flush with the street, and loose pieces of wood and concrete—a road improvement in progress on Nepali time. The driver maneuvers around these obstacles, stopping beside a gate. Inside, we see Amita, resplendent in kurta and matching scarf, a peach-and-white combination that perfectly complements her skin. In stark contrast to our dusty surroundings, she waits angelically on the other side of the gate to welcome us.

"You look beautiful," I say while smothering her in a maternal hug, and, after paying the driver, Paul follows suit.   Spreading his arms wide, he remarks, "Wow, Amita. You've really gone all out!"

The stairs lead us up the side of the building much like a fire escape. After three flights, we arrive at what looks like an open-air family room in front of a building with two doors. Clotheslines, flower pots, and a patio table and chairs fill the space. A black spiral staircase winds up another level to a platform adjacent to the roof that holds two water storage tanks and another clothesline. From here, we see across to other rooftop patios and apartments. A radio station and its transmission towers rise directly across from us, but not so close as to intrude. To the left, treetops jut skyward from the Jawalakhel Zoo.

Adam waits in the kitchen and steps out as we arrive. The smell of coriander and cumin follows him through the door. My nose wants to investigate, but Adam holds me back, guiding us in a different direction, and through a different door. Amita ducks back into the kitchen to resume her role as cook.

We enter a living area, which doubles as their bedroom. A desk sits in the far, right corner and a narrow bed sits to the left. Built-in cabinets and drawers store clothes and accessories. A bathroom sits to the left behind another door. Inside are hot water and Western bathroom fixtures.

Adam's apartment reminds me of the third-floor walk-up Paul and I rented in Berkeley before Adam was born. It also had its bed in the living room. At the time, Berkeley felt almost as foreign to me as Nepal does now, since we'd just moved across the country from the east coast. These thoughts put me immediately at ease.

In the kitchen, Amita is fully in charge. Several dishes wait to be served, and others simmer on a two-burner stove. Spice aromas fill the air, and the counter is replete with containers displaying various sources. One spice holder made of red plastic features molded wells, each with varying amounts of a different colored powder or seed.

Fascinated by the array, I say to Paul, "Look at this," as I pull him over to the counter. "Look at all these spices!" I ask Amita to describe each one of them.

Usually fluent in English, Amita has trouble remembering the English names, but with Adam's help she identifies some spices familiar to me, such as cardamom, cumin, and coriander. Adam takes a pinch of a different one and tells us to put a little of it on our tongues. It doesn't have a strong taste, but it makes the tongue tingle.

"This is what they call Nepali black pepper, or *timmur*," he says. "I really like it."

Adam pulls some bottles from a small refrigerator and pours drinks for us, then escorts us outside to take our places at the table. The sun is low in the sky and the temperature mild and pleasant. Soon, Amita comes out with her hands full of dishes. Adam jumps up to give her a hand. Between the two of them, they completely fill the surface of the table. She's prepared her version of dal bhat, and she's done it in style.

From left to right around the table, we have bowls of lentils, steamed rice, curried potatoes, stir-fried greens (locally known as *saag*), yogurt and achar (a spicy tomato condiment). It's too pretty to eat, so we don't eat it immediately. We take pictures instead. I intend to post them to Facebook as evidence my new daughter-in-law can seriously cook.

When Amita dashes back into the kitchen to get something, I say to Adam, "I'm not sure you realize what you have here. Amita can really cook."

"Oh, I'm pretty sure I do," he replies, the pride showing on his face.

I'm struck by the pleasure I get from seeing Adam in this new place. It lies in stark contrast to the sense of loss and betrayal I felt only last night. He has a right to be here enjoying this space, enjoying this love. This is what I've always wanted for him. I'm ashamed of how I doubted him, and how my selfish needs overpowered my caring for him.

Sometimes I wish I weren't his mother, that I could be just a friend, someone he casually passes on the street. I would be that nosy neighbor, butting into his affairs and asking intrusive questions of him. I probably wouldn't like that person, and neither would he.

Amita is that person who knows him as well as I, and she can love him in a way I cannot. She shares and embodies his love of Nepal, and I could never do that.

After we finish the meal, Adam insists on helping his wife with clean-up. This I take as a sign he has extended his egalitarian thinking toward the running of his own household. It remains to be seen how this works out for them in the long run, but they seem to be starting out on the right foot.

Paul indicated earlier that he needed a haircut. It's a tradition he started long ago when traveling overseas. Haircuts are always better and cheaper in other countries than in the States, and they often include shaves and massages for a nominal fee. After the meal clean-up is complete, we leave the apartment together and walk into Lalitpur.

Adam introduces Paul to his local barber who conducts his business from an open-walled shop. A slender middle-aged man with brown skin and thick black hair listens carefully as Adam describes the type of services he wants his father to have. The barber then beckons Paul to take his place in the barber chair. A massage and a shave will be included with the haircut, and it will cost all of 250 rupees—about US$2.50.

Paul's haircut will take about 30 minutes, and that leaves just enough time for Adam, Amita, and me to take a short trip to a nearby shopping district. We catch a taxi and, after only two tries, find a vendor who stocks the cell phone we want.

He's a very capable young man who knows how

to take apart and reassemble cell phones, as well as to completely set up a service for me in Nepal before we leave his stall.

For the equivalent of US$125, we bought a phone, two screen protectors, a phone jacket and SIM card. Later, when I have time to check, I find the same phone listed online in America for nearly twice as much, and I would have been forced to set it up myself.

Back in Lalitpur, we find Paul waiting near the barber shop shorn of excess hair, and looking relaxed and happy. Together we walk the local streets until we find a local woman selling stuffed pastry from a wheeled cart. Buying only a small amount, we eat it on the spot. The taste is unremarkable, but we enjoy the experience nonetheless.

I find myself living in the present through all of this, and leaving behind my fears. The unease and tension I harbored in the first few days have melted away like ice cubes on a warm summer's day. In their place is a new awareness, acceptance, and love. I can see it in Adam and Amita, and in Paul and myself. We're having a wonderful time, all made possible because none of our lives turned out the way we'd planned. Perhaps the unexpected is exactly what we need.

Tomorrow Amita will meet us again to go looking for a kurta I can wear to the wedding. I'll keep that happy thought in my mind and look no farther.

Chapter Five

TREADLE SEWING MACHINES

A morning walk into Thamel ends in front of a secluded garden restaurant. As Paul and I arrive, a woman in a dull olive and purple work kurta finishes mopping a section of the restaurant floor just to our right. She hurriedly rolls her bucket back to its storage place as we pass by.

A more tailored look adorns the young male attendant who pulls out a chair for me in the shaded part of a courtyard. Uncommonly early by Nepali standards, we are nonetheless treated with exaggerated respect. Paul sits opposite me, next to a broadly grinning golden statue of Buddha with white clown eyes. Mature Jacaranda trees partially block the sun appearing overhead, and staghorn ferns and split-leaf philodendrons build on the tropical mood. We order hot tea and masala omelets, and settle into a contentment rivaling the statue sharing our space. I sip my tea and think of Amita and our plan for today.

"I'm so excited to go shopping with Amita. This kurta will be authentic, not just a souvenir I bought in Nepal, and with Amita helping me, I won't buy something a local wouldn't be caught dead wearing. It will always remind me of our special time in

Nepal."

"Yeah, Amita's the real deal," Paul reflects. "She knows her way around the shops, and she knows what women wear. She'll also know what will be appropriate for you. Last night at their apartment, she proved she has excellent taste, both in what to wear and how to cook!"

Later, Amita finds us at our apartment still in a pleasant mood. We sit down while I show her a problem I'm having with one of my shoes. "We can have it fixed today if we find a cobbler," says Amita. She puts the shoe in a bag and insists on carrying it as we start out.

Lunch begins around noon in a third-floor open air restaurant in the Thamel District. Amita tells us the owner of the restaurant is one of Adam's former students. When he comes out to take our order, Amita introduces us. His name is Krishna, and he seems genuinely pleased to meet us.

"Adam taught me English for an IELTS exam five years ago," he says with a big grin. "Passing the exam made it possible for me to study in Australia."

IELTS stands for International English Language Testing System. As I look around me, I can see Krishna did well for himself in such a short time. His restaurant is not busy today, but it's furnished with about a dozen 6-foot rectangular tables that could accommodate over 100 guests at a busier time. I wonder how many others have benefited in a similar way by studying English in Nepal.

After we order our meals, Amita asks me again what I find wrong with the shoe. I show her where the tongue is fastened poorly and has a habit of migrating to the left or right instead of staying in place beneath the laces. Amita says she understands the problem and immediately excuses herself, saying only that she'll be right back. Our gaze follows her as she crosses the street, three flights below. She has taken my shoe to a nearby cobbler who sits with his tools on the sidewalk opposite the restaurant. We see Amita squatting beside him to explain the problem and suggesting how it might be fixed. Conversation continues while she stands to allow him to work. It takes him less than ten minutes, allowing Amita to return before our meal is served. I offer to pay for the repair job, but Amita refuses, saying the cost is virtually nothing and she is happy to help. It seems my mother-in-law status comes with some benefits.

Lunch is over by one o'clock, and we leave the restaurant promptly to complete our main task for the day, that of finding a kurta, or having one made. Assuming our familiar walking arrangement, Amita takes my hand to walk beside me, with Paul following closely behind. Early on, broad streets covered by asphalt and rimmed by broad sidewalks allow us to walk three abreast, but further along they become narrow and unpaved again with no sidewalks on either side.

As we enter the garment district of Thamel, a narrow unpaved pedestrian area appears before us, with open stalls displaying both ready-made and made-to-order traditional clothing. All the ready-made kurtas are packaged with complimentary scarves and trim to complete the ensembles. We stop at four stalls, all displaying bolts of fabric in riots of color. Shopkeepers are eager to please; they unfurl dozens of bolts of fabric onto the floors of their carpeted stalls to allow us to examine them. The fabric comes in virtually every color imaginable, from bright red to oranges, yellows, and greens. Some are made of dull cotton blends and some are made of more flimsy but brighter synthetics. Patterns go from straight geometric to Persian comma shapes with loops and curves. Only one merchant offers a cream-colored raw silk ensemble with dark purple trim. All three of us love it, so we soon return to that stall to allow negotiations to begin.

The kurta must be finished by Friday, only two days away, in order to allow time to pack it up and take it to Pokhara for the wedding. The middle-aged male shop-owner agrees to have it finished in time, but he will need to charge extra for that. We agree to a price that comes to about US$30.

Since I've sewn clothing myself in the past, I realize the amount of labor involved. We've saved a lot of money by not having such a garment made in the United States. Any custom fit ensemble for the mother-of-the-groom would have cost three times as much there.

With the price settled, the shopkeeper motions to a woman about his own age to gather the measurements. I feel like royalty as they wrap the tape measure around my torso and begin taking notes. Amita relishes the opportunity to apply her creative talents toward dressing me appropriately. She chatters excitedly with the woman in charge and turns to me to show the available shapes for the neckline and closures for the back.

"I like this design," she says as she traces her finger around a scalloped edge, "and I like a tie closure in back. It allows you to get it over your head easily."

I nod my agreement, telling her, "You know more about wearing kurtas than I do."

Colorful matching tights or more traditional pajama pants are worn under the outer tunic of the kurta. I choose the loose-fitting pants, which look better on someone my age. A small room, about 5-feet by 8-feet, behind the main shop serves as a privacy room for these types of measurements. I am now escorted into this room to obtain leg measurements. As I enter, I find myself drawn in by an attraction I can't quite explain.

Two young seamstresses, one cutting fabric on the floor, and the other sitting at one of two sewing machines smile shyly at me. The machines are the same vintage as my mother's Singer treadle machine I used as a child. These are prized in Kathmandu since they don't use electricity, and the city is known for frequent power outages.

I prize them for a different reason. Nostalgia overwhelms me, drawing me into this new setting that beckons me to sit with these two women and help them sew. Images form in my mind of happy gatherings of women, all chatting and sewing together. I see us drinking tea and telling stories... and just as quickly the images fade. The process of getting my measurements is completed.

Such a gathering will never happen for me. I am

not Nepali. I don't even speak the language. Feeling somewhat dejected, I rejoin the others, saying nothing about what I saw inside.

Paul wouldn't understand. It's just a "girl" thing, a memory of days gone by. He doesn't know what it's like to sew with other women, and has never used a treadle sewing machine. We arrange to pick up our order and leave the garment district of Thamel.

Exhausted by our morning of activities and the building heat, I suggest we go back to our apartment for a rest. We'll have tea heated on our own gas stove, and a snack of the cashews Paul and I picked up at a local shop. I welcome the opportunity to return some of the hospitality Amita showed Paul and I at her apartment last night.

Amita stays for about an hour, thoroughly enjoying the cashews as if she'd never tasted any before. She chats animatedly about her family and the upcoming ceremony, and uses her cell phone to message Adam about arrangements for tonight. I begin to believe happy gatherings, with at least this one woman, might be possible for me. Amita and I will probably never sew together, but we will do other things. We'll share a wedding ceremony, and she will come with us on a trek. We'll have those memories, and discover later what else the future brings.

I give Amita's hand a squeeze as we part again. We won't meet again until 7:30 this evening. Meanwhile, Paul and I will grab a quick nap. We're both feeling better every day, with diminishing jet lag and negativity banished from our thoughts.

Chapter Six

THE EXPAT COMMUNITY

Adam has chosen The Post, a trendy vegetarian haunt, for our venue tonight. It's frequented by expats like himself. An expat, or expatriate, is a person temporarily or permanently residing in a country other than that of their upbringing. As a mother, I regard expats warily since, by their definition, they avoid relationships that would tie them to their country of origin. Adam feels as comfortable in their presence as he does among his friends back in the States. He identifies himself as one, and has adopted many of their attitudes regarding nationality, giving it far less significance than those who have never lived abroad. Many expats never go home, but rather continue their vagabond existence indefinitely, having families and children in whatever country they are living at the time.

Attendance at The Post is mandatory on our part, since this is one of Adam's favorite haunts, and the evening is pleasant enough, except for our seating on the floor. That choice was optional, but the area is softly lit, and the atmosphere appealing for quiet conversation. Large pillows abound and low tables provide a conventional element to an otherwise Bohemian decor.

Paul finds it especially difficult to find a comfortable place to rest. Owing to a 40-year-old disc injury, his spine lacks flexibility, and he dreads any activity that occurs on or near the floor. He has propped himself against the wall with his feet stretched out diagonally in front of him. At first I am doing a little better, using pillows to help support a yoga sitting position I practice at the gym, but before long my legs too begin to ache. I straighten them in front of me, which means they extend under the low table in front of us and stick out about a foot on the other side. So much for pretense on our part.

It turns out that this restaurant is a great place for watching people, since the patrons here vary considerably from others we've seen in Thamel. As expats, they come in all nationalities, mixing and matching at random, having in common their youth, relatively affluent lifestyle, and proclivity for socializing. Adam points out several couples around us he has come to know, throwing a friendly wave in their direction as he does so.

Adam and Amita lounge comfortably, seeing no inconvenience whatever with their seating on the floor. They enjoy two frosty beers while swaying and bobbing to live music coming from another section of the restaurant. Paul and I are less into the music, but enjoy the ambiance none-the-less.

The scene is not new to us. In fact, we used to frequent a similar restaurant in San Diego, and loved the seating on the floor. That was many years ago, when the curmudgeon mentality of old age had yet to set in. We order *paneer* steak (a type of Indian cheese) and tofu kabob, and enjoy a cup of hot tea while unsuccessfully trying to appear young.

When the food comes, it's both appetizing and attractive, and at only $3 to $5 per entree, a real steal. If this restaurant were in California, we'd be paying four times as much to eat the same meal. But, while I enjoy paying these prices and eating this food, I can't help feeling threatened once again. With these kinds of attractions, Adam has no incentive to leave Nepal and move back closer to us.

I chew on my insecurities along with the food. If an expat is someone living, even temporarily, in a country other than that of their origin, then I am one as long as I remain here. I lived in Australia when Adam was little, and I surely was one then; I also enjoy traveling and the company of others who do the same. I believe people broaden their knowledge and viewpoint by living overseas. If all this is true, then I must try to figure out why this occurrence of "expat-ism" feels like such a threat.

My own parents resented my leaving home when I moved to California. I tried to impress them when they visited me in my new home, taking them to places I thought they'd find interesting. They responded by criticizing everything I showed them. "California is a desert," they said, as if that was condemnation enough. They were probably feeling like I do now.

Adam and Amita walk us to a street where we're more likely to catch a taxi. It's uncrowded and drivers mill around their vehicles talking amongst themselves to pass the time of day. At almost 11 p.m., this part of Kathmandu feels peaceful and safe. Compared to where Adam lived before coming here, this neighborhood is a paradise.

Saying goodnight, we climb into our taxi and head back to our apartment, each of us with thoughts to ponder on our own. I like to think of myself as lacking bias or prejudice of any kind, but lately I've been forced to examine the root of my fears. Change taxes everyone. Normalcy is boring and prevents personal development and growth. The young embrace change more easily, and adults grow less able to adapt with every passing year. Perhaps this difference divides us more than anything else, and determines if we are young or old.

Chapter Seven

THE HASH

The Hash House Harriers got their name in 1938 when British colonialists and expats began meeting regularly to socialize and run off the excesses of the night before. They ate at a local "Hash House" or dining hall in what is now Malaysia. The routine appealed to other expat populations and chapters eventually sprang up around the world. The "Hash" now defines a generation of like-minded expatriate individuals.

Adam's weekly running event with the local Hash is scheduled the morning after we attended a pizza and soda social with folks at our apartment. The gluten and non-nutritive sweeteners ingested were a small price to pay for meeting the owner's family and other residents. Still feeling queasy the next morning, I tried to beg off The Hash, telling Adam my stomach was upset.

"Mom," he said, "You can skip anything else you want during this trip, but you can't skip The Hash."

"Well, OK," I relented, "Just remember to bring the Imodium."

The required medication arrives with Adam, and

soon we're off in a taxi to The Hash. The ride there takes my mind off my churning stomach, and piques my interest as we wind our way through several neighborhoods on the outskirts of Kathmandu.

We arrive at an open field at the bottom of a hill dotted with homes. The homes vary considerably in design, but most are composed of concrete, painted pastel colors, and trimmed with at least one black metal railing. Flat roofs allow living space to extend outdoors, with gardening and clothes washing occurring on these upper levels. I climb out of the taxi, happy for the chance to breathe fresh air and stand on green grass after our time in the city.

About a dozen people mill around, tying on their running shoes, and chatting with others close by. Adam introduces us to Alicia, his IELTS teacher, and Tiffany, who works at the US Embassy. We meet Ray and his wife who are originally from Baltimore. They spent much of their life in Egypt doing medical work, raising their kids there.

Amita is wearing a new running outfit we bought for her at JC Penney. The words, "Too Fit to Quit" adorn the front of her T-shirt in fuchsia letters matching her shorts. They look good with a pair of FiveFingers running shoes we found on eBay and brought with us in our luggage. I wonder if it's a good idea to be wearing her new shoes before she's had a chance to break them in, but I overhear Amita tell Adam she's carrying her old running shoes in her backpack as a precaution. She's planned to change into them if the new shoes begin to bother her feet.

Adam is wearing his keffiyeh, a traditional

headdress of the Middle East. It's made of a black and white square of cloth folded and wrapped a particular style around his head. The keffiyeh suits him, beyond any practical aspect of providing shade. It accentuates his profile and imparts a foreign mystique. Adam's running shoes are made in Nepal, a point of pride where he's concerned. So fond is he of his "Made in Nepal" GoldStar running shoes that he brought several pairs with him to California last Christmas to give to his friends.

Fortunately for us, a small group of Hashers will be walking their route instead of running it. Having given up running several years ago, Paul and I are poorly equipped to do anything faster than a slow jog. We stay with the slow group, while Amita and Adam enthusiastically sprint up the hill with a group of ten runners.

Mercifully, our route is a gentle climb through wooded hillsides. Intersections of the trail are marked in chalk, but sometimes the chalk arrows point in two different directions. By tradition, The Hash includes routes with false turns and switchbacks designed to confuse. Seasoned Hashers who make up our group will decipher the messages for us and make sure we find our way. Our group totals eight people, including a seven-year-old boy who brought along his white terrier.

Since Ray and his wife are familiar with this region, they've decided to add another objective to our itinerary. It's situated just off the trail in a wooded neighborhood that lies just ahead.

After making inquiries of residents, they locate the shrine they remembered. It's a reclining Buddha, placed in the middle of a sixty-foot long reflecting pool. Entwined around his body are several slithering snakes carved into the stone; these are believed to protect him. Also protecting him are temple attendants who reverently adjust adornments and arrange flowers left by recent visitors. Captivated, Paul and I snap several photos before we resume our walk. We find it well worth the diversion, and take the time to thank Ray for the effort he put into locating it for us.

A disturbance seems to be brewing with the group just ahead. Apparently, the terrier has pulled free from his leash and gotten into a scuffle with the neighborhood cat. Distraught that his dog has taken off, the child wails, prompting Janet, the boy's mother, to hop a concrete fence in an effort to reclaim the dog. Since the dog is in no hurry to return, chaos ensues, and the scene plays out in comic disarray. To my relief, no onlookers materialize, and the situation quickly resolves itself before any damage is done or harm comes to the neighborhood cat.

Back at the staging area, cold drinks and appetizers await us on portable tables. Paul and I chew on cream cheese and celery and chat easily with others in the assembled group. Amita is one of the last to return. She took a wrong turn at one of the forks in the running path and had to use her cell phone to find directions back to the start. None the worse for the wear, she giggles at the applause her comrades give her as she at last trots into view.

Jake, a middle-aged Brit, is emcee of this week's Hash. He calls the assembled Hashers into a circle, and proceeds to lead us in beer-drinking songs. Most everyone knows the words to the songs, except Paul and myself, so we clap along as they sing. Irreverent and bawdy, the songs are designed to joke with, and embarrass, as many people as possible. The first to be pulled into the circle is a Nepali runner by the name of "Fuss." Fuss is toasted and roasted because he's planning to leave the group soon so he can travel and study abroad.

Next are Adam and Amita. Jake fills both their beer mugs to the top so they can be cross-examined in a good-hearted way about their recent marriage.

"Now, I'm never quite sure whether Adam is married or not." he chortles. "First, he plans to marry, and then he's not so sure. And now he says he's gotten married for good. But this time he's doing it up right and having a regular ceremony. Except everybody's going to know about it now, Adam. Mum and Dad are here, and there's no backing out!"

He claps Adam on the back and everyone sings "Drink, drink, to that!" Adam and Amita struggle to drain their mugs, beer dripping down their chins as they do. Laughing, and choking down the last few drops, they at last hold their mugs upside down as proof of their success.

By the time The Hash is over, everyone is feeling the warm effects of both the alcohol and the camaraderie. Tiffany offers us a lift back to our apartment in her UN Vehicle and we gratefully accept, knowing Adam and Amita have found their own ride home.

We sit in the back seat and reflect on the events of the day. "Paul, not only are international workers and expats exceptionally nice people, they know how to have fun. In addition, they make me feel like I am one of them, and that's a priceless gift when we're so far from home."

"Perhaps you are one of them, and perhaps Adam is one as well, because we raised him to be that way. Without consciously intending to, we've helped our son to feel comfortable in any community. There are worse things."

I smile at that. In this shrinking world, perceptions must, of necessity, change. Separate nationalities tightly controlled within strict borders have no place any more. Could it be, as John Lennon imagined, the world can now live as one?

Smiling again, I snuggle next to my husband, who led me to travel, and ultimately links me to all of this. Yes, a lot worse things could have happened in our lives than to have our son move to Nepal.

Chapter Eight

SPIRITUAL BENEFITS

Sunday in Kathmandu—a day businesses close in the United States, but not so here, and it's a good thing too. We leave for Pokhara tomorrow morning, and before any trek is possible, serious preparations must be made.

Paul and Adam take the lead in working out a destination, agreeing the most logical choice is the trail we started together seven years ago, the popular Annapurna Circuit Trail. It lies near Pokhara, the same site as the wedding. In 2007, we hiked west around the Circuit as far as Muktinath, but stopped short of the nearly 18,000-foot Thorong La Pass. We barely had time to hike that far and we also worried altitude sickness might be a problem on the pass.

This time we'll start at Besisahar, east of Pokhara and travel west around the Circuit. Since a road is now through to Mukinath, we'll take ground transportation from there back to Pokhara. That means we must make it over the pass, a feat Adam is confident we'll be able to do, since he hiked it by himself two years ago. Paul and I are less sure, fully aware of the physical disadvantages we face at our age. We're willing to give it a try and see how it goes once we're on our way.

A masala omelet at a nearby hotel suffices for breakfast, and we return in time to meet Adam just as he arrives. With checklist in hand, he strolls through the door, obviously primed for what lies ahead.

"Ready to go?"

Paul and I already have our jackets and walking shoes on. Around my hips, my leather waist pack resides, a less-than-chic security apparatus that holds all my valuables. We stand up in mock salute.

"Ready!" we respond in unison.

Adam swings his arm and bows in the direction of the door.

"After you."

I plant a kiss on his cheek as we pass by, never averse to wasting an opportunity to show some love, now that I'm here in the flesh.

A new pair of hiking poles will be among the first things we'll buy. Paul and I left our own in California to preserve luggage space, but we will need them for the sense of stability they provide on the more precarious sections of the trail.

We enter the district of Thamel as shopkeepers set out their wares for the day. At night, the merchandise is locked behind metal gates and roll-down doors, but now it takes its prominent place out in front of the shop. We pass tables full of brass goblets and bowls, and shelves loaded with locally grown tea. Down jackets in every size and color frame the openings of outdoor wear shops, and jewelry or luggage adorn many of the others. The unending variety keeps me vastly entertained.

The outdoor shop Adam chooses is no more than ten feet wide and thirty feet deep, and is open directly onto an unpaved street. It enjoys an international reputation, outfitting some of the world's top climbers. We wait, briefly gazing around at the hanging merchandise and overstuffed shelves. Another customer pays for his order before we step forward to ask about our poles. They stand partially hidden near the floor on the left, behind some down jackets. The shop owner pulls them out for us, and we choose two each of red and black. They cost only US$8.00 a pair, which is ten times less than we'd have paid in the States, and since they're spring-loaded, they may be less jarring to use.

Paul and I weren't planning to rent sleeping bags, since we hadn't needed them on our previous hike in Nepal. Every guest house along the way offered a stack of blankets to keep us warm, and we brought along the same set of flannel liners to put between us and the bedding provided. Adam and the shopkeeper disagree with our strategy; since we now plan to climb as high as 18,000 feet, the stakes are much higher this time.

When asked if we need to carry sleeping bags, the shopkeeper rolls his eyes, but states his opinion clearly enough to be understood.

"You only need them if you want to live."

Paul and I look at each other and swallow.

Adam looks at us and shrugs, saying off-handedly, "I can carry them for you."

Ever mindful of Adam's youthful advantage, Paul

surmises what the extra weight will do for us in terms of slowing our son down. Adam is not recovering from an illness as he was during our last trek, so he'll have twice our speed and energy. Paul joked with me earlier about putting a few rocks in Adam's pack.

Now Paul shares with me, "The sleeping bags might work better than rocks. Seriously," he continued, "they'll also provide an extra measure of insurance. You never know when a freak snowstorm will show up out of the blue."

Turning his attention back to the shopkeeper, he says, "We'll take two medium-heavy weight sleeping bags, please." Neither of us can justify loading Adam down more than that.

Next order of business is the paperwork we need for the trek. Adam finds a digital studio on a busy street corner near our apartment. They make passport photos for our entry permits and TIMS cards. TIMS stands for Trekkers' Information Management System, and it's the way Nepal keeps track of foreign trekkers. The TIMS card will be stamped at several stations along our route to ensure a record exists of the last place we were seen.

At a local travel agency, we find a man we recognize, and he welcomes us as we walk in the door. After a short wait in an outer room, Laxman welcomes us into his office.

"Welcome, Adam," he says. "Come in and tell me all about your plans for a trek." He bows toward us. "And these are your parents. I believe we've met before."

"Seven years ago," says Paul. "Adam was living in Pokhara at the time."

Turning to Adam, the travel agent smiles. "And now you have a Nepali wife. Tell me about her. What's her name?"

"Amita," responds Adam. "She stayed at home today to prepare for our wedding."

"Oh, so you're having a ceremony?" he says while clapping his hands. "And your parents will be here to take part in it. How wonderful for you."

Laxman's office assistant, beautiful in a red and green sari, delivers green tea for us. We sit back in our chairs with cup in hand, now ready to return to business.

"The TIMS passes won't be ready until tomorrow," he says, "but I can have them prepared in Pokhara where we have another office. You'll have plenty of time to pick them up before your wedding."

"Have you arranged for a guide?" Laxman asks next.

Adam looks startled, and replies, "No, do we really need one? I've already hiked this trail by myself."

"It's regulations now," he says, "but I think you have an advantage in Amita. Since she is Nepali, she can be your guide."

Adam chuckles at the thought of it, and says "Amita has only been on one other hike with me, and she has never hiked the Annapurna Circuit Trail. Now you are suggesting she be our guide. That's quite a step up for her, yet I see the wisdom in your proposal. Guides are expensive, and it would save me a lot of money not to have to hire one for this trek. Why don't you call her and see what she says? She needs to know what to do when she's on the trail."

Laxman dials the number Adam gave him and Amita answers. They speak in Nepali while Paul and I quietly sip our tea. When Laxman hangs up, he reports triumphantly, "She'll do it!"

Smiling, Adam chimes in, "I'll bet she really liked the part about free dal bhat." Turning to us, he explains. "Most guest houses along the trail offer free food to guides in order to attract foreigners to their lodging."

As the ramifications set in, he straightens in his chair. "Hey! That'll cut my food bill in half. Amita can eat a lot!"

All of us laugh at that, and the good mood continues as we wrap up the details. Before long, Laxman wishes us well and sends us on our way.

"Now don't forget to stop by and tell me how it went," he tells Adam, and slaps him on the back.

Paul and I wave good-bye, thanking him vigorously before exiting the door, but as we descend the stairs and step out onto the street, a drop of water hits me on the head. Looking up, I can see the sky has darkened and conditions are now ripe for a shower. We pull our hoods up on our jackets and prepare to get soaked. During the call to Amita, Adam was reminded he promised to rent her a sleeping bag liner. Since he forgot to do this, we turn back in the direction of the shop we left earlier.

Ducking into doorways and weaving back and forth, we shelter under the few awnings found along the way. When Adam notices a pedal cab coming toward us with its canopy up, he hails the driver and hops on board. Next, he reaches down and pulls me up to sit by him. Another pedal cab goes around us and he shouts to Paul to hire that one. Hesitating for only a second, Paul climbs on board and leads the way down the narrow street.

At first, I hold onto Adam's arm for support, unsure whether this is a good idea or not. The street is bumpy and crowded with pedestrians more intent on avoiding the rain than stepping out of our way. We swerve right, then left, pause, and start again; I find myself beginning to laugh aloud. There isn't any danger of seriously crashing into anyone, because we're moving too slowly, yet the jerks and starts are strangely amusing. Yes! I'm enjoying myself. This is more fun than a carnival ride!

By the time we reach the trekking store, tears of laughter stream down my cheeks. Mixing with raindrops, any distinction is erased, so all one sees is a huge grin on my face. Flushed and smiling, we pay the driver and dismount, asking him if he'll pose for pictures before heading out. This experience might have been missed were it not for the rain. I find myself feeling grateful for the cloudy day.

The rain dissipates as we conclude the last of our business, and we walk back toward our apartment with relative ease. We're forced to step carefully, though, as large puddles now exist where none had before. A bright turquoise sari with matching slippers floats by us, skillfully avoiding the newly laid mire. Following her, whole gaggles of brightly dressed women pass by seemingly unscathed. I'm astounded by their beauty and grace in the face of such a muddy mess, and wonder how they can possibly cope during the height of the monsoon.

The streets eventually lead us back to our apartment, where a puddle the full width of the street blocks our way. In line behind those who've done this before, we hop onto a narrow strip of curbing that offers the only dry route to the broad elevated sidewalk ahead. Bearded men smile and nod in our direction uttering friendly Namastes. We reply in kind, aware that a grumpy temperament is inappropriate where so much peace and contentment exists.

Our Sunday chores reaped spiritual benefits for us, though none were anticipated as we began. We received friendship and helpful assistance at the travel agency, kind level-headed advice at the trekking store, and laughter and mirth in the street amidst a drenching rainstorm. These positive encounters warm the soul and raise our spirits as we prepare to enter the mountains of Nepal.

Chapter Nine

THE BARBECUE

At the apartment, I sort my meager belongings for our trip to Pokhara. They must be pared down to what fits in half a small suitcase and one of two hiking backpacks. Bibek has graciously offered to store our large bag nearby until we return to Kathmandu, but I'm still unsure about what I should take for the wedding.

My kurta turned out well, but I can't wear it to everything. And my hair—it will look downright hopeless without the benefit of a hair dryer. I stuff my makeup case in the corner of our shared overnight bag as furtively as a squirrel stashing his prized nut for the winter.

Gesturing toward my leopard print sateen pajama set, Paul says dryly "You won't miss it on the trail, and nobody's going to see what you're wearing to bed in Pokhara." I toss it onto the pile for storage, and move on. Amita's family will see the real me. Not much room for pretense around here.

Catching the bus to Pokhara will pose no

difficulty for us; the bus stop sits directly in front of our apartment. We merely need to awaken in the morning in time to meet Adam and Amita beside the proper bus to take us there.

The greater challenge belongs to Adam and Amita. Not only will they need to pack everything for a wedding and trek, they must also clean up their apartment after entertaining twenty-some guests tonight, then prepare to be away from home for a full two weeks.

Knowing this, Paul and I approached their apartment with some concern earlier in the day. Adam was still with us, having hailed a cab after we finished our errands. Paul and I wondered how Adam and Amita would be able to pull this thing off. Certainly, we wouldn't have the energy to entertain the night before leaving for a wedding and trek, but Adam and Amita seemed to have no such limitations.

"Don't worry, Mom," said Adam with an air of authority. "We got this thing covered."

Amita met us at the door with a big smile.

"Here, let me take your wet coats" she said, helping us slip them off and hang them on a hook by the door. "Have a seat and I'll be back as soon as I've finished in the kitchen."

To my amazement, Amita seemed to have everything under control.

We took a seat on the couch and looked around the room. It was totally changed from when we'd seen it before. Amita did an impressive job of arranging chairs around the perimeter of the room and placing thick carpets on the floor. The room took on a bohemian flavor similar to the one we'd seen at The Post only a few days before.

Worsening weather threatened their party from the start. Showers like the one we'd experienced earlier in Thamel continued, totally inundating some sections of the city. One of Adam's guests called to say waist deep water had him trapped outside his office building.

Even so, guests began to arrive at the appointed time, and Adam fired up his charcoal burner in the kitchen and opened the windows wide. He had planned for barbecued chicken, and a little bit of rain wasn't going to get in the way.

As each new guest arrived, Adam quickly introduced them to us, and then ducked back into the kitchen to finish grilling. We were the center of attention, the honored guests, while Adam and Amita practiced being hosts. The guest list read like an international "Who's Who" of foreign workers.

Bursting through the door about 4:30 were Sabina and Joyce. They were soaking wet, but quickly shed their jackets and hung them to dry. Sabina, we quickly learned, hails from northern India and works with Adam. Her friend, Joyce from Scotland, has lived in Nepal for about 20 years.

Next to arrive were Mark and Anne. Mark is from the Netherlands and Anne is from Colorado, but Anne gained her citizenship in the Netherlands before they moved here.

Sabina's son, Rajesh, arrived next. Only fourteen years old, he was shy and reserved in this environment. Rajesh's father is a Norwegian development professional living in Egypt and working for the United Nations Development Program (UNDP). Headquartered in New York City, UNDP provides advice and training to developing countries.

Shajahan is a former interpreter from Nepal, and Teresa, once on the Peace Brigades International (PBI) team, now works for the National Women's Commission. Rajika, a former restaurateur, is a friend of all the girls on the PBI team. (PBI is an international organization known for protecting human rights defenders by providing unarmed accompaniment. Adam worked for PBI while developing his incident tracking website.)

As Paul and I conversed with Adam and Amita's friends, we learned more about the rewards and challenges of living overseas. They provided context for what Adam's life has been like since moving to Nepal. Properly impressed, we wondered if the effect was intentional, a conspiracy between Adam and his friends to win over the visiting folks from back home—it worked well for me.

Adam's chosen lifestyle is good for him. His friends are open-minded, and well-educated, free of the insular thinking I'd seen in some localities back in the States. He thinks globally, as a citizen of this planet, rather than of a particular city or state. I'm comfortable with this knowledge, knowing Paul and I don't have to fix anything. He's doing pretty well for himself.

Of course, there are trade-offs. Global thinking has the effect of distancing a person from the people and places they call home, but, to be truthful, Paul and I set the example ourselves. We lived as virtual vagabonds while Adam was young, moving twice in California and once to Australia before settling down when he started school. It's no wonder that Adam has trouble identifying with any one family or place.

Fewer people attended the barbecue than expected, so lots of food was left over at the end of the affair. After offering as much as she could to her guests, Amita called in the neighbors for help. Before her guests left, two women and a girl of about thirteen years descended on the kitchen with extra bowls and plastic bags. They were busy helping Amita tidy up the kitchen as Paul and I said our goodbyes and climbed down the wet metal staircase to the street.

My smart-phone lit the way to a row of taxis parked a short walking distance from their apartment. Now comfortable with negotiating our way alone in Kathmandu, we were still mindful that some cab drivers are known for charging foreign travelers more than the going rate. We took the precaution of asking Adam how much we should expect to pay before we left.

Paul approached a group of drivers standing outside their cabs with his offer. "Four hundred rupees to Kantipath?"

Since the bus station is located in that part of Kathmandu, all the drivers know where it is.

The third driver in line swung open his door. Sighing with satisfaction, I slid into the back seat. I was relieved at the prospect of returning to our apartment with enough time left to pack our bags for our trip to Pokhara tomorrow.

Part 2

POKHARA

HINDU WEDDING AND FAMILY

Chapter Ten

THE ROAD TO POKHARA

At 8 a.m. we step on the front sidewalk, now flanked by a row of buses the length of a city block. After searching through the growing crowd, we find Adam and Amita standing by a bus, about two thirds of the way down, marked "Pokhara." Sidewalk vendors pester us to buy sweet rolls and bottled beverages. We approach one of them, but Amita intercedes.

"Don't buy anything" she says, "I've brought along leftover barbecued chicken and *buff* (dried marinated water buffalo). We'll have more than enough to eat."

Strangely, beef is not eaten by Hindus, but water buffalo is a favorite food. "It's because cows are regarded as a source of food," Amita explained, "not food in themselves. Cows selflessly provide milk, cheese, and yogurt for us. The least we can do is let them live out their lives peacefully. We treat them much as you do your dogs and cats in America."

We choose seats across from each other near the

rear of the bus. Other riders include foreign travelers, as well as local Nepalis. Many seem well accustomed to traveling by bus, and have brought along snacks and water bottles similar to our own. Some women are well-dressed in colorful saris, while others wear blue jeans or more functional kurtas. Functional clothing isn't as bright, and the fabric is plain cotton, with fewer decorative details around the edges. Almost all the women wear their thick black hair long, falling loosely around their shoulders or tied up fashionably on top of their heads; hair ornaments keep their luxurious locks in place. As in America, men dress plainly, but also wear traditional attire, such as topi hats and their version of the kurta, a tunic-style shirt.

As we settle into our seats, I see Amita answering questions from curious onlookers about her foreign-looking traveling companions. She isn't shy about telling them of her wedding plans, and the Annapurna Circuit trek to follow. They seem genuinely happy for her, smiling, and clapping her on the shoulder as they wish her good luck.

As the bus begins to leave Kathmandu, Adam exchanges a few pleasantries, nodding and smiling in support of Amita, but before long his droopy eyelids show how drowsy he is. Placing a fleecy jacket under his cheek, he curls himself around Amita's petite frame, allowing the sleep that eluded them both last night to overtake them now. Their mouths gape open in unison, instantly signaling to those around them a need for quiet and rest.

I can't help staring at them as they sleep. If I had any doubts about whether Adam and Amita enjoy a close relationship, this candid posture put it to rest. They nestle together as one, like two cats reclining on a couch, exceedingly comfortable against their almost vertical seat back. I don't begrudge them their well-earned rest, instead mentally caressing them as I watch. Bumping Paul with my elbow, I cock my head in their direction. We both look at them and back to each other, sharing a moment of affection for them both.

The view from the bus keeps me entertained. Green-terraced hillsides are framed by mountains in virtually every direction. The temperate climate nurtures banana and fig trees that spring forth in groves along the roadway. Every area of flat land is tilled for growing food by farmers using hand tools. Oxen can be seen pulling plows and women carrying heavy loads on their backs. It stands in contrast to the large-scale agribusinesses we see back home.

After taking in the scenery for several hours, I finally begin to doze, only to be startled awake by a loud crack coming from beneath the bus. "What was that?" I mumble aloud, and hear the answer from a young man about two seats back. "I think we have a flat tire," he speculates, his Indian accent revealing where he may have gained this insight.

The bus pulls over to the side of the road in a large parking area. The driver investigates and confirms the Indian passenger's surmise. We're instructed to get off the bus and stretch our legs while the tire is being changed.

Since I passed up an opportunity to use the meager toilet facilities at the last stop, I am now in dire need. I discreetly share this information with

Amita, who quickly discovers there's a public toilet available for paying customers in a small white stucco building to our right.

As we approach, smoke rises from an outdoor roasting pit, and two women wearing aprons step back to offer us a place to sit. Large rectangular tables with folding chairs lie barren under a tarp. We take a seat while Amita orders milk tea. Before the woman has a chance to step away, I ask my one-word question, "Toilet?"

She pauses, then points at a small wooden doorway, and I bound off in that direction. As expected, it's not fancy, but much appreciated just the same. The light from my smart phone becomes indispensable when I find myself in total darkness once the door is closed. A bottle of Purell I keep in my pocket suffices for absent sanitation.

No sooner have we finished the last drop of tea than the bus is ready to go. We hop on board and start down the road only to hear about another possible delay. Adam reads a text on his phone from a friend in Kathmandu who reports hundreds of travelers are stranded due to mudslides in the nearby Chitwan Province.

We're not sure if the mudslide is ahead or far behind us until thirty minutes later when the traffic slows. After the bus stops completely, we disembark in a rural area flanked by green rice fields. Passengers begin to mill around and stand in various postures along the roadway. Paul pulls out his camera to make the best of an unexpected event.

A well-dressed group of Nepalis stand by the front of the bus, and Amita tells us they're a wedding party. She uses the opportunity to describe the clothing they wear.

"The groom is the one wearing the gold-colored topi," she said, "and around his neck is what we call a wedding garland." It's a wide yoke, bordered by a grassy green fringe. "The bride is the one in red," she said, "and she wears a lot of gold and precious gems."

"What a day to have a traffic delay!" I say with concern. "They might miss their own wedding."

"Oh no," responded Amita. "That is probably not the case. This trip is part of their procession, and it will only continue after they arrive. Most weddings last about three days. They'll be fine, and the delay will not affect them at all."

An interesting approach to a wedding, I think, remembering brides I've known in the States who drive themselves mad on their wedding day. Exorbitant costs, logistics, and issues around who's on the guest list often doom a marriage in the United States before it has a chance to begin.

We walk with Amita toward the wedding couple and offer our congratulations. I'm unable to understand very much of what is being said, but Amita gushes over the bride's costume and admires her jewelry. Paul and I stand back and smile politely, then ask to take their picture. They seem flattered and willingly oblige.

Seeing movement in the line of traffic ahead, the driver signals for us to climb on board. The elation we feel is short-lived, quickly degenerating into a calm tolerance, as we and our fellow passengers endure a slow crawl for several more hours. No roads exist for detouring traffic. Our only option is to wait until road crews have fixed the road ahead where the mudslide occurred.

When we reach the mudslide area, we see a single lane bridge hastily put into place on top of the fallen debris. Deep furrows scar the brown dirt-covered hillside above, and water running downstream from the slide is thick with debris. Two excavators and a backhoe operate at full capacity. More work must be done before traffic can pass in both directions. Our bus slowly passes over the narrow bridge, and we pick up speed, finally released from our torturous delay.

In the end, a trip that was supposed to last seven hours took a full fourteen hours to complete. A dinner we had planned with Amita's family had to be canceled when it became clear we wouldn't be able to make it on time. Adam and Amita conveyed our regrets by cell phone when we realized how far we still had to go.

The bus pulls into the Pokhara station well after dark. We're left with an utter lack of humor about our long ordeal. Nothing to do now but make the best of a shortened evening that remains.

Chapter Eleven

LAKESIDE

Pokhara is Nepal's second largest city in terms of population (about 500,000), but covers an area larger than Kathmandu. Lying just 120 miles west of the capital, it varies dramatically in elevation from north to south. Lakeside, the part we plan to visit, sits at just 2,700 feet, but other parts of the city reach as high as 5,700 feet as it draws closer to the Annapurna Range, only 15–35 miles away.

Bus station workers pass our bags down from the top of the bus. Satisfied everything survived our fourteen-hour ordeal, we strap on our backpacks, and begin wheeling our remaining luggage toward a distant sidewalk. Designed for asphalt, not dirt and loose stones, they bounce and fight us all the way to where a line of taxis sit waiting for their next fare.

Amita and Adam take the lead, conferring with a group of taxi drivers, while Paul and I stand back guarding the bags. Negotiations don't seem to be going well, and heated words are exchanged. Amita charges back in our direction, grabbing her bag.

Hoisting it over her shoulder, she exclaims "They don't want our business."

Adam follows after her and instructs us to start walking down the street. Paul and I remain clueless about what's going on, but we pick up our bags and follow.

Two of the cab drivers follow us and plead with Amita to reconsider. She shouts back her demands. They hesitate, and she continues to walk away. Paul and I are beginning to catch on.

An inevitable price is struck, and we pile into a single cab, but Amita is not finished venting her rage. She continues to rant at the driver from the back seat for nearly five minutes into the ride. Paul and I steal looks at each other and can't help being amused. Amita is showing a lot more spunk than we'd given her credit for.

"Yeah," I chime in, "What she said."

Paul grins and whispers, "Shush, you'll make it worse." Then we both privately giggle.

After watching our antics, Adam explains, "Pokhara is Amita's home town, so she's particularly annoyed to get the kind of treatment she did. She's brought her new in-laws home with her, only to find cab drivers trying to scalp us with inflated charges. It's a personal insult in her mind."

Adam seems disappointed, as well. He's lived here too, while teaching English at the local academy. This is where he met Amita. Used to being recognized as a local, this greeting seemed less than friendly to him.

Arriving in the Lakeside District, I feel myself

begin to relax. Paul and I spent a lot of time here on our first trip together to Nepal. We stayed in the same motel, appreciating the charm this community offers and its slower pace.

Adam owned a motorcycle then, a Classic Royal Enfield that he adored. His social group included the guys at the local repair shop, where they rebuilt parts of it damaged when it slid down a hill. Fortunately, Adam wasn't sitting on it at the time, and he came through the accident virtually unscathed.

We hung out with Adam at his local repair shop, drinking tea and watching cows lounging nearby and ambling undisturbed down the street. This was his neighborhood. He was comfortable here, and he wanted us to see it that way, too.

Adam took me on a ride through a nearby valley, allowing me to hang on tight behind him as we passed by golden rice fields where farmers winnowed their crops and gathered straw into tall mounds. That memory ranks high among those I treasure most with my son.

Now, checking into our rooms, we greet the staff like old friends. Adam knows them well, having lived with them for most of the time he was here. It was nice of them to wait up for us, since we are arriving so late.

After greeting us warmly, the family also lets Adam know during the course of the conversation that they are disappointed in him. They had counted on an invitation to his wedding, and have been hurt by being left out. Adam explains the ceremony will be very small, and includes only family members, but feels uncomfortable knowing he's committed a serious faux pas.

Dealing with this new situation adds to emotions already raw from our experience with the cab drivers, leaving both Adam and Amita too keyed-up to think of going to sleep. The four of us decide to go out for a drink at an establishment Adam knows, only a short walk from here.

We step into a balmy evening, the street quiet except for an occasional burst of noise from the odd motorcycle going by. Closed tourist shops line both sides, their metal security gates locked down tightly for the night. Above them, light leaks from the windows of scattered restaurants, sometimes spilling fully out of open doorways, but otherwise the street is dark, silent, and restful. I relish the ease of walking here compared to the tangled clatter of Kathmandu.

A large tree occupies the middle of this thoroughfare, a remnant of days gone by when two-story brick and mortar buildings didn't exist on either side. It still offers shade for weary pedestrians and lounging cattle during the day, and tonight for motorcycles whose owners prefer this spot to other spaces along the curb. We pass by the tree on our left and hear Persian music coming from the restaurant upstairs on our right. A pale Western couple strolls by in blue jeans, like us, holding hands and enjoying the mood. We smile and they nod back silently.

Arriving at the bar and restaurant, we find the inside devoid of customers, but many remain outside on wicker patio furniture. Low glass tables hold food and beverages, and some sport tall water pipes for smoking flavored tobaccos. Faint wisps of tobacco smoke hang in the air. Our open-air ceiling is filled with stars.

Paul and I order milk tea and a dessert of cooked sweetened apple and rice while Adam and Amita order burgers and fries, along with a water-pipe of apple-flavored tobacco. I lean back on my seat cushion and lift my gaze to the sky. Stars shine like beacons against a sea of black, the constellations obvious as a child's coloring book. I pick out Orion and the Big Dipper before Adam shoves his cell phone in front of my eyes. It, too, shows me the constellations, but they're labeled. I grab the device out of his hands, intent on a thorough examination of the night sky.

"You can do that, too." he declares. "Your phone came with that app installed." Inwardly, I prepare for my latest IT lesson, knowing resistance would be futile. Stargazing remains my preferred activity.

"Oh really," I say, showing feigned interest.

"That's why we got you a cell phone with GPS capability. It's called Google Sky Map. Here, let me show you."

I cooperate with Adam, knowing how he loves anything techy, but soon the meal arrives to rescue me, and we settle back in our seats and talk about other things.

Relaxing and magical, the environment nurtures us for another two hours. Other tables empty one by one, the chairs being stacked on those around us, until the restaurant workers ask us to take our leave. They've had a long day, and so have we, and a bigger day waits for us tomorrow. The wedding looms large in front of us as a tantalizing celebration.

Chapter Twelve

THE WEDDING CEREMONY

Adam and Amita make a grand entrance into the cafe. His gray hand-tailored pinstripe suit accentuates Adam's six-foot frame, and Amita sparkles beside him in her red and gold sari. Heads turn as they stride toward our small table in the rear.

My eyes focus on the details of Amita's bridal attire. Dozens of red and gold bracelets cover her wrists, and the backs of her hands dance with intricate designs drawn in reddish brown henna. Under a fine red veil, she wears her black hair loosely around her shoulders, offsetting wide dark eyes and brilliantly red lips. More sparkles adorn her face. Silver dots draw an arch above two perfect black eyebrows meeting in the center at a red and silver star, her esoteric third eye, or Hindu seat of wisdom. Finally, sitting discreetly on the side of her delicate nose is a tiny gold nose stud. Smiling broadly, she places both hands, palms down, on the table in front of us.

"We painted my hands last night," she said. "I painted my left hand because I am right-handed, but I couldn't paint my right hand, so Adam had to do that. He painted the solar system on it."

I smile at this. Adam has a strong interest in astronomy, so it makes perfect sense. I trace my finger over the back of her hand, following the spiral lines trying to identify which dots represent which planet in his solar system.

"Adam, it looks like you left out Jupiter," I say in jest. In truth, I can't make out anything I recognize. "How long will the henna last?"

"About three weeks. It's more of a social custom than a religious custom, but henna on your hands represents an expectation of happiness. I could have them on my feet, too, but we were too tired to paint them last night."

"I'm amazed you found time to do all that you did," I say. "I was exhausted last night." Looking down at Amita's sparkling red sandals and her red painted toenails, I add, "I'm sure you will have lots of happiness in your marriage, even if you haven't painted your feet."

A taxi driver waits for us at the curb. Twenty minutes later, he delivers us to the north side of Pokhara just outside the Bindyabasini Temple Complex. A concrete wall surrounds the complex, which sits on the top of a hill. Stone steps and a metal railing lead us upward. Since the lighting is in our favor, I ask Adam and Amita to pose for pictures on the way. We get one shot of them climbing the stairs and another of them standing at the top. I stare at the vision they present, not wanting the moment to end.

As parents, seeing our son in this setting is beyond what we could have imagined. For years, Adam had vowed he would not marry, so we hadn't dared to hope he would change his mind. Now he has included us in the ceremony. I quiver with excitement as we mount the stairs. Tears wet the outside corners of my eyes; I scold myself for forgetting a handkerchief. Gripping the scarf of my kurta, I steel myself against emotion, not wanting to yield to maternal feelings of loss.

Focusing instead on Amita's family, I feel a growing sense of unease regarding how we'll be received. Will they be friendly, or only polite? I'd have a better sense of this if we had been able to join them for dinner last night. The landslide had prevented us from meeting them and possibly breaking the ice. Now, we meet for the first time today without knowing how they feel about being part of our family. Did they plan for her to marry someone else? If so, they might not approve of what's happened now. I cross my fingers as I enter the complex.

In the center of the complex sits a two-story white fluted dome on a raised platform. Smaller pagodas and shrines cluster around this main temple in a park-like setting. Trees offer dappled shade and crows and pigeons fly overhead, their droppings mixing with the dampness of the darkened concrete to produce a slightly musty odor, successfully masked by wafts of incense emanating from the surrounding shrines. South Asian men and women in formal dress stroll throughout the grounds, talking quietly among themselves, intent on a spiritual experience of their own. Bindyabasini is one of the oldest temples in Nepal and revered worldwide by Hindus and tourists alike.

Amita leads us to a simple pagoda about 20 feet square with mushroom-shaped cutouts in its low open wall. Shoes line up in veneration outside. We slip ours off, stepping up through an opening in the wall onto a bare concrete floor.

The pagoda is attended by a young priest, wearing orange robes, his assistant, and five members of Amita's family. Introductions aren't possible yet, but I recognize Amita's family from pictures she has shown me on her cell phone. Our focus is immediately drawn to the ceremony.

Amita takes a decorative collar fringed in grassy green and places it around Adam's neck. He does the same for her. These are the wedding garlands, and exchanging them represents a blessing and purification. In arranged marriages, it also represents mutual consent to proceed with the ceremony. Since this ceremony was anticipated eagerly by both bride and groom, no permission is required. I breathe a sigh of relief.

With smiling eyes, Amita's Aunt Padmini and mother, Leena, approach Paul and me with multiple ceremonial scarves. Both women share the eyes and coloring of Amita, making them instantly recognizable to us. The orange and white khatas symbolize compassion, and are given only by those with a pure heart. Draping them carefully around both our shoulders, the women assure us all will be well. In addition, they crown Adam and Paul with identical Dhaka-patterned topi*s*, and add another layer, a matching shawl, to my shoulders.

Sufficiently festooned, we are gently led by both women to a metal garden bench set off to one side. My earlier trepidation is dispelled, replaced by calm and gratitude as we are incorporated into the ceremony.

The priest, his straight long hair tied behind his neck, and with only a small tuft of hair on his adolescent chin, looks barely sixteen. His assistant, younger still and a full foot shorter, wears a lighter colored full-length robe and covers his head with a Mideast-style orange and red scarf. Like actors in a Sunday school play, they begin to administer the rites of marriage. I wonder about their qualifications or level of experience to do so.

Those thoughts fade as soon as the priest begins to chant. He sings a mantra in Sanskrit so flawless and so pure that I recognize the seasoned scholar in him. His melody sets the stage for the ritual events to follow by providing a continuous stream of sacred background music. At the same time, and without coaching, his diminutive assistant bows at the feet of the wedding couple to present them with their set of golden wedding rings.

Molded of gold from a chain presented to Amita long ago by her father, the new wedding rings represent not only a bonding of their love, but a reminder of cherished memories gone by. Her father lived for too short a time, but is remembered here through the soft and wide-eyed expression on Amita's face as Adam places the ring on her finger.

Another ring ritual begins soon after. The holy

grass ring ritual is performed around the fire pit in each of the four directions, each direction honoring a different deity. A grass ring is placed on Adam's finger, and the priest sings a mantra to Lord Shiva facing north.

We watch as the ritual progresses slowly, methodically, in its clockwise direction around the circle. I recognize similarities in the four directions with rituals performed in California among Native Americans, and around temples we visited in Bali. I settle into my seat, comfortable with my place in the universe, and my right to be here among these people who worship in this way. The cadence of the mantra feeds my soul.

Adam and Amita take a seat cross-legged on thick red patterned carpets to our left and well within our line of sight. They face the fire pit where they will light the sacred fire and feed it with continuous offerings. Flower buds and brass containers of rice, milk, and honey circle the fire pit. Other containers made of leaves for holding more organic offerings are grouped in a display in front of them; all are arranged with loving care and minute attention to detail.

At the appropriate time, Leena steps behind the wedding couple to open a cloth bag full of ceremonial items. She helps Amita light a small copper oil burner shaped like Aladdin's lamp, which Amita and Adam then carry to the center of the fire pit where a pile of wooden sticks stands ready to ignite. They return to sit at the fire pit in front of *Agni,* the Hindu god of fire.

Amita's brother, Parakram, in a blue shirt and

black pants has an important role to play, as well. With his hand-held camera, he is the official photographer, and from where I sit, I see that he's serious about this duty. At times, squatting and stooping, at others bounding swiftly but quietly to the other side, he records all aspects of today's experience.

Parakram also plays a part in several rituals. He accompanies the wedding couple as they begin their journey into married life by circling the fire four times. At one point, he ceremoniously places a bundle of rice into Amita's hands with Adam's hands cupped around her own. She will open the bundle later before throwing several grains into the fire.

In another ritual, the bride's mother pours holy water onto Parakram's palms, which flows into the groom's and then into the bride's palms, symbolizing the continuity of life, and the passing of the family heritage on to the next generation.

Paul and I sit quietly on the sidelines taking our own pictures and intently watching what is going on. We notice onlookers gathering outside the pagoda. They may be curious about the mixed-race marriage taking place inside. I see them gesturing in our direction and quietly talking among themselves. Just as Amita shared her wedding details with the people at the cafe, these onlookers receive a briefing from Amita's aunt and mother across the low wall that separates them from us. Knowing nods and friendly grins result, as the news is passed around.

Adam and Amita apply a thick paste of rice and vermilion to each other's foreheads. The so-called *tikka* is then given to them by several members of the wedding party and by us. Since this is the first time I've applied a tikka, I'm awkward and tentative. A spill will leave permanent stains on clothing and anything it touches, but encouragement and patience in the eyes of my new in-laws sustain me, and I prevail. Both Paul and I receive generous applications of tikka in return, resulting in tikka on my glasses, and tikka on our camera, but these items are made of plastic, their surfaces only enhanced by red traces that will remain as cherished reminders of this event.

The wedding party follows the bride and groom to the main Bindyabasini Temple, a white pagoda-style structure trimmed in red and gold. It sits in the middle of a wider brick platform that stands about three feet high. Steps lead up to a doorway in the front, behind which the goddess *Durga* presides. Durga is regarded as Pokhara's guardian deity, known for granting wishes.

A long line of Indian pilgrims wait to make their own offerings. Cutting in front elicits only a polite question from the person behind me as to my country of origin. My one-word response echoes down the chain of humanity one person at a time, "California, California, California, ..." all the way to the end.

Here, Amita receives another application of vermilion, this time to the parting line of her hair. *Sindoor* is put there, in this case by her husband, as the mark of a married woman, and then covered with a patch of white cloth to shield it from the eyes of others. Hindu tradition considers married women to be full of color, while widows wear no color on their face at all. (Amita's mother ceased wearing color at her husband's death, and cannot look on her daughter's sindoor today.)

The brief Sindoor-Dana ceremony is followed by a slow amble clockwise around the upper ledge of the Bindyabasini temple. Imitating Amita's mother and aunt, I strike the clapper onto the side of three fixed brass bells, the solemn ringing of which pulls me over the edge of my barely controlled emotion. With each clang, I say goodbye to the fat baby that suckled at my breast, the tow-haired toddler who clung to my legs. Gone are the three of us curled up together on the couch, reading or watching TV. He belongs to another woman, another culture now. A lump as big as a fist rises in my throat, and tears cascade down the sides of my cheeks. Abandoning any further effort at composure, I surrender to my predetermined destiny and weep.

Chapter Thirteen

TYING THE KNOT

"My name is Parakram. I am Amita's brother."

Looking back at him, I blink through my tears and present him with an inelegant wet smile. Of all the first impressions I could have made, this one has to be the worst.

"And this is my fiancée, Sadhika."

"Pleased to meet you," I say weakly, wanting to say more, but unable to get past the lump still lodged in my throat.

"I'm sorry," I finally spit out. "It's hard for me to talk right now."

Out of the corner of my eye, I see the rest of the wedding party regrouping ahead and about to return to the wedding pagoda. Using it as an excuse, I make a break in that direction while chiding myself. I justify my cowardly act as necessary to put myself back together and regain control.

Adam and Amita now sit in the seats we formerly

held in the pagoda, and Leena squats before them, apparently setting up to wash their feet. I gather around with the rest of the wedding party as Leena positions herself in front of a brass basin set on a green mat on the floor. She holds a brass urn finger-painted with red and yellow stripes, and is settling into a perfect flat-footed squat. Her perfunctory movements suggest easy familiarity with the ritual. Family members offer encouragement, as if she were doing something as ordinary as cutting a cake.

Adam and Amita suspend their bare feet expectantly over the basin. Amita giggles as the water hits her feet, while Adam exhibits a more circumspect attitude. He's aware of the honor this represents. Since he is not a practicing Hindu, in the eyes of those who are, he is an outcast, and Amita has broken caste by marrying him. In fact, in religious settings such as this, many Hindus might feel compelled to reject Adam as a suitable mate. Instead, this woman honors him by washing his feet.

Adam formally gained acceptance several weeks ago in a traditional tikka ceremony held at the family home. He had given and received tikkas from family members in the past, but one person had not participated. Parakram, as the only male, remained to decide the matter. His application of tikka to Adam on that day sealed the deal, and paved the way for making further plans toward matrimony.

Government paperwork has already recorded the marriage of Adam and Amita, but a part of the wedding ceremony remains that makes their marriage legal in the eyes of Hindu relatives. The sacred "Seven Steps" represent seven sacred vows believed to strengthen their union. While a priest chants, the couple circles the fire seven times, allowing Agni, the god of fire, to bear witness.

Adam's interpretation of circling the fire blends traditions of East and West, demonstrating to all observers his level of commitment to his bride. Instead of merely carrying her over the threshold, he will carry her seven times around the fire, promising with each circumambulation to keep another vow.

Pausing before picking her up in a cradle hold, Adam takes a big breath in a mock attempt to pump up his muscles. The priest, clueless at first, seems confused, then smiles broadly as Adam dramatically swoops Amita off her feet. The priest's incantation suffers only a few brakes in its flow while he stifles a laugh, or pauses to take in the happy event playing out in front of him.

The first vow promises nourishment, the second promises strength, and the third promises prosperity. Adam sweats more profusely with each turn around the fire. Amita is laughing uncontrollably, obviously flattered, but perhaps a little embarrassed by her husband's presentation. Family members and bystanders cheer him on, as he strains under his lovely load. The fourth vow is for wisdom, the fifth for progeny, and the sixth for lifelong health. Cameras flash from every direction, as onlookers capture the color of their costumes and gaiety in their laughter for all time.

Finally, Adam rounds the fire a seventh time, and in doing so, promises his wife they will be lifelong friends. He can now release her. His arduous journey is complete, but unbeknownst to him, he's been put at a disadvantage for the ritual yet to come. In addition to being physically exhausted, Adam has been left clueless about the purpose of the next ritual.

The tying of a symbolic matrimonial knot always follows the Seven Steps, and the outcome of this ritual determines who will be the decision-maker of their family. Amita has told him nothing about it. Innocently, he watches as she places the rice pouch in a long strip of cloth which they will both pull taut, enclosing the rice bundle in a large knot. Adam has no idea it's a tug of war for dominance.

Amita deftly plays her part, pulling hard at first, then letting Adam take up some of the slack. Finally, she pulls hard enough to tip her unsuspecting husband over onto his side, amid cheers and laughter from the surrounding crowd.

Amita let's Adam in on the secret, once he's been had, but if he harbors any ill will from this catastrophic defeat, he doesn't let it show. He happily assists Amita to her feet, and they exit the pagoda triumphantly as husband and wife.

The sun is shining, but haze and humidity hang in the air, leaving Machhapuchhre Peak, famously visible from the temple complex, still shrouded in clouds. The background for our group photos defaults to the temple complex itself, which includes the main temple, along with several other pagoda-style shrines made of brick with tile roofs. The spicy scent of sandalwood *Dhup* (an extruded incense) freshens the air.

We take photos from every conceivable angle,

sharing cameras back and forth between shots as necessary to make sure no family member is left out. I'm placed most often in the front flanked by Amita and Parakram, which I take as a compliment. Both of these people are prominent in my new family, and it makes me feel special to be placed between them.

A planned picnic starts immediately afterward, in a shady spot near the perimeter of the complex. Leena and Pashupati have brought an insulated carry bag full of *aloo dum* (spicy potatoes), *sel roti* (fried rice doughnut), and thick yogurt. All are made with rice flour, which fits nicely into my gluten-free diet. Seated comfortably on the perimeter wall next to Amita, I balance a paper plate on my lap.

"I told my mother and aunt you don't like to eat foods made with wheat flour," Amita explains. "It's no problem in Nepal to find foods that are made without it."

"But this is so delicious!" The pungent aromas of garam masala and cloves fill my nostrils as I sink my teeth into soft chunks of potato.

After a pause to swallow, I continue, "And I really appreciate you taking my needs into account. It's such a treat to be able to eat freely, and not worry about whether there's something in the food I shouldn't eat."

Off to one side, I notice Leena sitting by herself under a nearby tree. Half expecting to learn about a strange Hindu custom, I ask Amita, "Is there a reason why your mom sits over there alone?"

"No," she responds, and then she calls out to her, inviting her over to join us.

Sensing my opportunity, I pat the seat beside me

on the wall, indicating she should come sit next to me. No translation is necessary.

Immediately, the sad expression leaves her face, as she picks up her plate and virtually skips across the open space that used to stand between us. She's been waiting for an invitation. What had she been thinking? Doesn't she know how grateful I am she bore this child? We are connected by the bond of motherhood as surely as if we'd known each other from the start.

Together we devour the food, made more sweet by the company we keep. We are two moms, a favorite aunt, and a shared daughter. Do they know I would already kill to keep her safe?

Amita and Leena see me only as Adam's mother, and now we share the bond of family ties, but there's so much more. My heart is scarred, just as theirs are, by the ravages of womanhood. I take comfort in being among them, but knowing the details isn't necessary. All women pay a price. We're in this together, gaining strength from the successes of others among our ranks.

Leena and her sister, no doubt, see a success in Amita marrying someone of her own choosing, someone who promises to be good to her, and help her to grow. I won't be a cruel mother-in-law, and if given a chance, will probably do what I can to help Amita succeed. Perhaps it will take time for them to believe this. They have fears, as well as hopes, as I do. For now, they let me see only hope.

Chapter Fourteen

THE FAMILY HOME

Adam and Amita return to Lakeside with us so we can change into casual clothes. After a short stroll around town, we take a taxi together to Amita's family home. It's the evening of their wedding day around 6 p.m.

Leena opens the front door and welcomes us into the family room. Two padded benches with slipcovers lie at 90-degree angles to each other. While a variation of the upholstered furniture I'm used to seeing, I recognize their more functional value. With a little more bedding, the benches double nicely as additional sleeping quarters, and the nearby porcelain sink with mirror, up one step and to the left of the entryway, adds another nod toward efficiency.

After consulting with her mother, Amita tells us, "My mom is preparing a special dal bhat meal for us in the kitchen, but it won't be ready for an hour or so. My brother and I will take this time to show you around."

We follow them to the second-floor landing where, tucked into a small alcove, the family altar provides a space for daily prayers and offerings. Pausing to light a candle there while we watch, Amita kneels and presses her hands together in front of a 12-inch tall statue of Ganesha, the Hindu deity with an elephant head on a human form. Lord Ganesha represents the Supreme Being capable of removing obstacles and ensuring success in all human endeavors. Hindus worship Ganesha first before beginning any religious, spiritual, or worldly activity. Today's wedding satisfies every criterion.

"An altar is a place that helps you connect spiritually," Amita says upon rising, "or to concentrate your energy for any purpose. It usually changes with the seasons or to reflect changes in you as a person."

I suspect Amita's altar has changed many times since meeting Adam, each one recognizing changes in herself and the deity. Unlike my son, Amita wears her spiritual identity on her sleeve, unapologetically enacting each ritual, as though it were part of her, which it undeniably is. As a mother, I'm comforted in knowing at least one of these two members of my family attributes a deeper meaning to life.

The next flight of stairs deposits us on the rooftop, where the family enjoys sunshine, breezes, and a great panoramic view. The surface is flat and smooth as a patio, but its purpose goes far beyond relaxation or entertainment. A clothesline stretches across the right side, and containers of gardening soil and tools lie scattered about.

Parakram points to a row of clay pots, saying,

"I'm propagating poinsettias and geraniums here. Tomatoes I've saved from last year are just beginning their new growing season. These plants over here still lie dormant. Ideal gardening temperatures won't arrive for them until next month."

Walking to a handrail near the edge, we look out to see the boundaries of their property, and where the boundaries had been before their father became ill. The degree to which the property shrank following his death illustrates the consequences they suffered in the aftermath of this event. A Nepali family, absent a male adult, has no source of income. More than one hundred discriminatory laws place women in a position subordinate to that of men.

"Parakram was barely out of diapers when our father died," Amita explains, "and our mother struggled for many years to keep our family afloat. Until Parakram became old enough to earn money, selling parts of our property was among only a few options open to her."

A separate residence occupied by their aunt, Padmini, and her daughter, Basanti, sits to the rear of the main house. We walk past their doorway on our way to a building in the back. Parakram, now fully grown, runs a new enterprise here.

Having checked first to make sure we won't disturb any paying customers, we enter through a side door into a large room set up with two billiard tables at right angles to each other. Patrons come here regularly to play pool; his business has now grown to a point where it provides a steady income for the family. We walk around the ample space outside a perimeter created by the billiard tables. Parakram describes in detail artwork and photographs decorating the walls.

"This is a place designed for folks to hang out and play pool," he tells us with pride, "or they come to just socialize with neighbors and friends."

As if on cue, relatives and people from the community begin arriving, one at a time or in groups, failing to disguise the fact that a large gathering had been planned here in advance. Thirty or so people of all ages introduce themselves to us, posing for pictures and explaining their relationship to the family. All would have been wedding guests if the wedding had been a larger affair, but this private venue suffices nicely to provide the perfect opportunity for us to meet them. As they mill about, Amita and Parakram act as official translators for us. Cameras flash and exchange hands with all imaginable combinations of group photos taken by all.

After about an hour, Padmini arrives to tell us our dinner is ready. We say good-bye to our well-wishers, genuinely thanking everyone for this splendid opportunity to meet. With smiles and friendly waves on both sides, we leave through the same door from which we entered, following a well-worn path back to the main house.

Small by American standards, Leena's kitchen is none-the-less charming, accommodating a round table just large enough for four chairs. Two kitchen essentials, the ubiquitous two-burner hot plate and a pressure cooker, fill much of the counter space, and a small fridge sits off to one side. A brass mortar and pestle appears to be the only other special cooking tool, yet we'll be fed well and in grand style.

Leena sets a round metal plate the size of a medium pizza pan in front of each of us. She piles the middle high with white, fluffy rice from the pressure cooker, then begins filling in the space around it with colorful accompaniments. Tender pieces of spicy chicken are followed by mounds of cooked greens, a small bowl of liquid dal, and spicy potatoes. Colorful achar is the last to arrive, as we're enveloped in a cloud of heavenly aromas from fresh chopped ginger, garlic, and cloves.

Leena watches as we eagerly set to eating, attentive as a maître d' at a fine hotel. We consume small amounts, only to have them replaced soon after when she offers more. Adam, used to eating large quantities of food, is eager to comply, while I'm more reticent, holding my stomach and wondering how I'll ever manage to clean my plate. Several times I shake my head "no," hovering my hand over my plate to guard it, but then relent when she offers achar, the pickled vegetable accompaniment still caressing the back of my throat.

At one point, I suggest to Leena that she sit down to join us, but she makes clear her role is to serve, and ours to eat. Remembering a more typical Nepali wedding lasts a full three days, I begin to suspect this ritual meal is part of a grand ceremony in Leena's mind, meant to help join our two families together and solidify our relationship. Savoring my last three forkfuls, I concede the tradition has its merits, and succeeds in producing the desired effect.

Leena can barely remember a time when she wasn't caring for others. Her own mother, partially paralyzed following Leena's birth, was placed in her care from an early age. As a result, Leena couldn't attend school, and after her own husband's death, she also raised two children alone.

Paul and I meet Leena's mother a while later when she's invited to join us in the family room. Her progress into the room takes an enormous effort, but no one jumps up to help her along. She's done this before, and takes pride in being able to move on her own.

Inch by inch, she drags her mangled body by sheer determined will. Muscles that work pull along those that do not, her body doubling over as though weighed down by an invisible force. Having made it to the end of the couch on which we sit, she looks up with a toothless grin, while her grand-daughter begins the conversation by translating the introductions.

She calls herself Jayati, which means "victorious," but life hasn't been easy for her. A tumor the size of a fist occupies the right half of her lower jaw, having started many years ago when an episode of ill-fitting dentures went without sufficient medical help. The condition grew worse until a minor infection became something more, and now the time for any permanent remedy has passed. Breathing and swallowing are sometimes difficult. Her speech is significantly impaired.

Jayati stays for the rest of our visit, knowing she belongs here with us. Were it not for her disability, she would have been in charge of everything that happened on this day. As head of household, she would have been at the temple, and she would be overseeing the operation of this home. Instead, she depends on others to do what she cannot.

As we prepare to leave, Amita's aunt, Padmini, tells us, "It's my turn to cook for you after you've finished your trek. I share in the responsibility to make sure you're all well-fed."

I smile at that, knowing being "well fed" means far more than simple nourishment. It's further confirmation and acceptance of us as a part of their family. We are two people of whom she knows little, but chooses to honor just the same.

While I look forward to the original purpose for our trip, that of taking a trek, I've found this part to be especially gratifying. My mindset at the beginning of the wedding festivities focused on losing a son, but instead I've gained a warm welcome into an extended family. I feel a connection to all of them and have committed to an ongoing relationship. We are truly part of Amita's family. There is no separation between her family and us. In fact, we are one and the same.

ANNAPURNA CIRCUIT TRAIL MAP

PART 3

THE TREK

GOING FULL CIRCLE

Chapter Fifteen

POKHARA TO BESISAHAR

Bus seats are never guaranteed in Nepal, not even when you purchase a particular seat, not when you arrive early, and not when you place your belongings on your seat and go out to have a cup of tea. Ours are occupied by two Nepali women, a mother and daughter dressed in red and yellow printed kurtas and bright yellow scarves; they tossed the items we left on those seats carelessly across the aisle. Adam politely approaches the women and, in his best Nepali, asks them to move so we can sit down. They refuse.

Fully expecting the bus company to make good on the seats we'd purchased, Adam shows the driver our tickets. The driver pretends this is the first time such an incident has ever occurred. He tries to convince Adam he is powerless to intervene. Only after complaining to several other drivers and the bus station attendants does Adam finally recover our seats. Such persistence rarely pays off in Nepal, since catering to the needs of individual passengers is not the norm.

As Adam negotiates these details, Amita disappears down a nearby street intent on procuring enough snack mix from local vendors to sustain us for the remainder of the day. Such precautions would seem frivolous elsewhere, but after our experience traveling here from Kathmandu, we've learned short bus rides sometimes turn into much longer ones devoid of opportunities for buying food.

We leave Pokhara with a full bus, or so we think. Every seat is taken and Paul and I sit comfortably in a seat about midway on the left side. Amita and Adam are behind us with only a seat back between us. Here we can share snacks back and forth and easily talk to each other. I find the circuitous route we take strange given our full load, until the bus begins to stop and load on more passengers.

The first ones sit on supplies and luggage stacked in the front, and those that follow perch on wicker stools pulled from the overhead shelves and placed in the aisle. A burly man with a broad back places his wicker stool next to me, encroaching both into my space, and that of the woman sitting across the aisle from me. One disgruntled passenger refuses to board the bus when he discovers his bogus assigned seat, while others seem more resigned. The last passengers stand in the open doorway and sit on the steps when the door is closed. Only then does the bus take a turn onto the main highway, triumphantly blasting music from its sound system to announce the driver's success at loading the bus past its designed capacity.

Among surrounding passengers, I see other

trekkers, but as expected, most are less than half my age. At least I look the part, dressed as I am in hiking shirt and pants, the grandma of the bunch, and Paul the seasoned senior citizen. I surmise we're dismissed by the others as too old for serious hiking and likely to turn around before the going gets difficult. Their youth and bravado will tell them no one over the age of sixty could possibly do as well as they.

In fact, their relative youth has been found to be a risk factor for acute mountain sickness on treks such as this. It's not that the physiology of older people is superior—because it's not—but people under the age of fifty often lack the necessary judgment when it comes to showing caution. They may, for instance, fail to go down in altitude when symptoms present. They feel invincible in their young bodies, until after it's too late.

Which one of our group of four will have health challenges before this trip is over? It probably won't be Adam, because he's the strongest and has made this trip before. He hiked it on his own only two years ago, finding it to be "quite doable" for the rest of us. Since he's our unofficial leader this time, Adam may be a bit naïve about potential outcomes for the rest of us.

Adam assumes Paul and I can finish the hike because we did well seven years ago, but now we're both older. The likelihood we'll develop problems has only increased. I'm not having issues with my knee anymore, and Paul's hip isn't bothering him, but a whole host of other ailments remain to threaten a successful trip. Amita, as the youngest, is expected to do well, but she isn't immune. Her new hiking boots could produce a blister, or she could come down with a cold.

Looking around our overcrowded bus, I realize how lucky we've been so far. Our stomachs haven't given us issues while on these long rides. Bathroom stops are rare, and being packed in like sardines isn't helping us. It would be nearly impossible to get out of here in a hurry if we needed to.

Mercifully, Besisahar materializes after about three hours, before any emergency stops. The bus disgorges us, along with the rest of the passengers, onto a dusty street. Buildings around us stand two and three stories high, with shops and businesses located at the ground level. As in other parts of Nepal, sidewalks don't exist, but paved areas sometimes border the street next to larger establishments.

We stand briefly in front of an open-air butcher shop until the smell of dried blood forces us to move away. Our backpacks lean against our legs while we decide what to do. It's time for lunch, so Adam volunteers to hire a jeep for four people while the rest of us secure a seat in the dining room of a nearby hotel.

While we happily down our favorite curry and rice dish, the young jeep driver Adam hired hunts for more passengers. In this region, jeep trips might not happen at all if no foreign travelers materialize to pay for the gas, but once that's taken care of, additional passengers provide both profit and companionship for the driver. Friends ride for free if there's room, and if the friendship is close, it doesn't seem to matter whether any space actually remains. Paying customers are forced to bear the discomfort of riding with their knees against their chest to accommodate, powerless to prevent the intrusion.

In keeping with this tradition, we arrive on the scene. An exclusive ride is impossible. Adam and Amita protest, but to no avail. The driver assures us we can all fit in the rear seat along with our packs, which we eventually manage to do. Four local people sit in the front on two bucket seats, and three men climb on the roof. The driver has met his self-imposed standard. We are simply part of a typical load of passengers for a jeep ride to the town of Chamje.

Many hikers avoid the problem of overloaded jeeps by beginning their trek here at Besisahar. We don't have that luxury, since part of our allotted trekking time was reassigned to the wedding. Taking a jeep shaves two full days from the trekking portion of our trip and helps us catch up with our original schedule, but not without leaving us feeling deprived.

As we pull out of Besisahar, I peer longingly over Paul's backpack at a group of three male hikers blissfully embarking on the first section of the trail. They'll walk along the roadway at first, then take a separate and unspoiled route along the Marsyangdi River. We'll see the same river, but often at a distance, and over the edge of a precipitous cliff that marks the side of the road.

Chapter Sixteen

BESISAHAR TO CHAMJE

A short distance out of town, our jeep driver brakes suddenly when he spots police in the road up ahead. Three sharp raps on the metal roof send a signal to the roof-riders to scramble down the side. As they secretly scamper off into the woods, the driver pays a 200-rupee bribe, a sum no-doubt fully accounted for in the price we paid to hire the jeep. The riders magically reappear half a mile up the road to resume their perch on the jeep top, a momentary stop and knowing smile on the face of our driver the only acknowledgement of their right to be there.

As tourists, we are unwitting accomplices in a system of corruption designed to stretch our tourist dollars as far as they will go. Not only have we provided transportation for six additional people, we've also padded the salaries of local officials. Our contribution to the economy becomes more apparent the farther we go, and it's become increasingly obvious we have no say at all in the matter.

The jeep makes slow progress on the rough and bumpy road, first offering wide views of the Marsyangdi Valley, but then progressively climbing through steeper and more narrow terrain. Only wide enough for one vehicle to pass, the road is littered with boulders both recently fallen from the cliff face above, and partially embedded in the road surface beneath. Tucked tightly in the close quarters of the jeep, I hold my breath in terror regularly, as we veer too close to the edge, yet find each episode then tempered by stunning vistas and pastoral scenes in the landscape far below.

Green hillsides are chiseled into terraces and dotted with modest wooden dwellings surrounded by sheep and goats. Waterfalls spill forth into streams, joining the Marsyangdi River as it snakes its way through an expansive valley. People we see along the roadway show gradually darker complexions, more closely resembling Tibetan natives who for decades have entered Nepal whilst fleeing China across the nearby border. Women are clad in horizontal striped woven aprons and carry their children in slings on their backs. Increasingly, we see wooden hand tools and oxen being used to till the fields.

Amid plentiful sunlight and mild temperatures, we reach our goal in Chamje at about 4 p.m. At 6,000-feet above sea level, the altitude mimics winter ski venues in the Sierra Nevada Mountains in the United States. We've traded the subtropical climate of Besisahar for one more typical of a mountain town.

Chamje itself is a short block long cluster of buildings; most are three stories high and decorated with white wooden balconies on the second floor. They rise on either side of a narrow street paved with wide flat stones, no doubt borrowed from the river that flows in the canyon below. The first hotel and restaurant we enter offers us free rooms if we take our meals there, so we agree to stay.

That decision we regret a few moments later when pungent aromas of curry emanate from a rival accommodation across the street. Never mind, we've chosen to stay with a charming family that indulges our greatest wish by serving a pot of hot lemon ginger tea with local honey on a terrace overlooking the gorge. They agree to let us take their picture; a round-faced grandmother, mother, and two friendly teenagers, their faces showing Tibetan heritage. After they show us some ornaments they have on display and tell us about their family, we no longer feel we've missed out.

The terrace is about eight feet wide and thirty feet long and covered with a corrugated tin roof. We sit on stackable plastic chairs on either side of rectangular red tables. When Paul leaves the rest of us to take a walk in the canyon, I feel emboldened to talk about subjects that matter to me.

Adam and Amita share their plans for the future with me. They include Amita attending college, which I wholly support, but I worry they might run out of time. It's a defect exclusive to persons of maturity like myself who recognize the finite aspect of life. Delaying reproduction can get in the way of achieving what I consider to be crucial life goals.

"You know, Adam," I say with authority while Adam rests his arm across the back of Amita's chair,

"It would be better for Amita to have her first child before she reaches the age of thirty. It's just easier on a woman's body to go through childbirth at a younger age."

Adam rolls his eyes and straightens in his chair. I brace for a lecture about overstepping my bounds, but it doesn't come. Instead, he wears a tired smile and looks me straight in the eye.

"No pressure, Mom. You know it'll take several years for Amita to get through school, and she doesn't even have her visa yet."

"Yeah, I know. Sorry. I just wanted to get that in there, for what it's worth. Life has a way of playing tricks on you. It doesn't always give you everything you want when you want it.

"Well, you're right about that, but, hey, I got married, didn't I?"

"Yes. Yes, you did, and that's a big part, so I'll be quiet now and just be happy for you. I'm still basking in the glow of being the mother of the groom. That was special, very special. Thank you."

Then looking straight at Amita, I add, "Thank you both."

We lean back again and resume sipping our tea, my mind going to a place where we can all be together again as an expanding family. I would be the doting grandmother, and they the frantic, but loving parents. But, alas, my reverie is interrupted by an all too familiar reality check.

In ten years, I will be seventy-five, not capable of caring for children anymore. If I'm still around, it will be too late for me to fully participate as the grandmother of my dreams. My own words echo to the exclusion of all else: *Life doesn't always give you everything you want when you want it*. Prophetic, but perhaps negative.

I look fondly across the table at the two people who give me so much. Dare I expect a traditional family life, as well? It's not likely, and perhaps too much to ask. The existence of grandchildren would have already precluded what we're doing here today. I have the best daughter-in-law I could ever want, so simply appreciating this fact might be in my best interest right now. Let the future play out on its own.

Chapter Seventeen

CHAMJE TO TAL

The first suspension bridge stretches tightly across a narrow section of river just a ten minute walk out of Chamje, at the bottom of the gorge. It flexes little underfoot, and waist high mesh sides provide additional stability, a protection not needed here where the height and sway offer no challenge. I stop mid-span to admire the rounded boulders only 20 feet below. Oh, that my first suspension bridge seven years ago had been this easy to cross; it was not.

That 350-foot span stretched across the Kali Gandaki River Gorge near the town of Tatopani. In 2007 I wanted to turn around and abort the trip when I saw it. Bedecked with several strands of prayer flags, it brought to mind the tattered ropes and missing floorboards of an Indiana Jones bridge, replete with crouching tiger at the other end. I shook off that image, seeing instead stainless steel with thick wire cables on its sides, but the difference was barely discernible. A thin band of metal formed the floor, swooping down low toward the river gorge, and swaying gently in the wind before returning to its mooring on the other side. It terrified me.

Paul, Adam, and I were staying in a dormitory-style guest house below the bridge, well within sight of it. Adam confirmed early that evening we'd be crossing here the next day. I told him I wasn't sure I could do it. He argued that I must cross it, as though he were scolding a child. I might have found the role reversal amusing at another time, but I wasn't laughing then.

Adam reasoned the bridge was very strong because mule teams walk across it. We watched as two dozen mules approached, each lined up and tied to the next, carrying what looked like a 200-pound load. They ambled across without hesitation, an astonishing feat, given their reputation for stubbornness. I couldn't imagine doing such a thing, let alone on four legs. I was afraid I'd freeze in my tracks, unable to move forward or take a step back— but I was wrong.

The next morning, heart pounding, I approached the bridge. I would be the one to go first. The bridge bounced and swayed proportionate with the mass and vigor of the person (or mule) who walked before me. My hiking poles were useless, since they'd get stuck in the cracks of its see-through floor. I held them horizontal in one hand, the other hand free to grab the side, although doing so would be a bad idea. It would probably throw me off balance, and, worst of all, betray my anxiety to other hikers coming from behind.

Strangely, I cared about what other hikers thought of me, and wanted to look good in front of my husband and son. Perhaps I feared bringing shame on the family. The absurdity of that thought had me seriously questioning our relationship, but I lacked the time and courage to deal with it then. Instead, I stepped onto the bridge.

My heart lodged in my throat and my breath drew shallow and weak. It was like walking on a tightrope, with no net below me. I could spread my feet wide, which I did, as long as doing so didn't interfere with precious progress moving in a forward direction.

"Forward, keep moving forward. Walk, keep walking, keep breathing, keep your eyes open, look ahead, keep moving, walk...," my words, spoken in hushed tones, were immediately swallowed by the rush of water below where certain death awaited me.

A slow decline gradually became a gentle incline, barely perceptible at first, but it meant I was past the half-way mark, and then three-quarters of the span. Finally, my feet touched solid ground again; I wanted to kneel down and kiss it, but didn't dare. That, again, would have made me look foolish. I cared what my "guys" thought of me, and wanted to be strong. I didn't know the reason then, and still don't know why.

We shared hugs and high fives when Paul and Adam joined me, but my jubilation was short-lived. The process would repeat again before we reached the next town. I found the second bridge easier for me, and the third easier still, until seeing a suspension bridge didn't make me panic any longer, and like the mules, I took them pretty much in stride.

Here I am, on the other side of the Annapurna mountain range, seven years later. I stroll across this first suspension bridge unaware of what lies ahead. Six hours of hiking stand between us and Dharapani, a destination more than seven rugged trail miles away, but only 1,500 feet higher. In our favor are mild temperatures and a sky mostly clear and sunny, though haze and clouds on the horizon still hide the snowy peaks from our view.

My backpack rides well, balancing perfectly on my hips, its weight shared equally with my shoulders. It weighs half what my son's pack does, even before he added our two extra sleeping bags. Adam's pack extends well above his ears, making the rest of us, by contrast, feel like lightweight day-hikers.

Protected well under long sleeves and a broad-brimmed hat, I'm ready for a day in the sun, but Amita wears a sleeveless shirt, and Paul's ears sit dangerously exposed beneath his light nylon cap. Adam wears a red and white checked keffiyeh, the soft cotton cloth provides no shade for his eyes. It's all I can do to keep from mentioning my concerns to each of my ego-driven males, but I know it wouldn't play very well.

I'm expected to leave the "mother" role behind in settings like this, and be just one of the "guys." The fussing and straightening and cautioning I exhibited while guardian of my son's young life is no longer

appreciated here. Men look for bravery and
defiance, two emotions unnatural to me. It's the
price I pay to accompany them here.

Dirt crunches beneath my feet, turning my
attention to a familiar burning sensation just behind
the fourth toe of my right foot. A Morton's neuroma,
new to me since hiking in Nepal the last time,
promises to reduce my foot to a throbbing pulp by
the end of the day. Multiple visits to podiatrists and
five years of wearing prescription orthotics have
yielded little improvement. Two cortisone shots, a
last-ditch attempt to prevent pain, were injected just
days before I left the United States. It remains to be
seen whether they will make the difference I seek.

We come upon a crude shelter, with a thatched
roof supported by rough wooden poles, overlooking
an impressive view of the gorge. The trail widens
between it and the small dwelling belonging to the
teahouse proprietor. Each of us carries a bottle of
purified water in our pack, but additional fluids are
needed to ensure we won't run dry. Although the tea
is unremarkable, tea tastes much better than the
iodine-treated water we brought along. We also
relish the opportunity for precious shade and rest.

Camaraderie comes from a group of German and
Polish hikers who arrived shortly before we did.
Four in all, two men and two women, all in their
twenties, travel together. Both women wear shorts
and tank tops, oblivious to the burning rays. We take
stock of how we're doing and share the sunblock
around. I notice the skin of one of the German girls
just starting to show pink. Projecting my repressed
maternal instincts onto her, I point to her shoulders

and pass her a bottle. She gratefully accepts, releasing those instincts temporarily from their exile.

Up the gorge, we see steep hills covered in green grass beginning to give way to jagged peaks where soil no longer clings. One tall cone-shaped spire towers a thousand feet or more above the surrounding rock, with a tiny line chiseled into its face. The line spirals upward from left to right climbing relentlessly toward the top.

Recognition turns to awe, then astonishment, when we realize the line we see is a road blasted into the side of the spire, the same jeep road we would have taken today if we hadn't walked this route.

"Oh, my God," I breathe as I admire not only the monumental effort it must have taken to build such a road, but also the colossal courage required to actually use it.

"I don't think I want to come back this way by jeep," I say, the harrowing episode that was yesterday's ride still fresh on my mind.

We all agree we don't need the added excitement of tackling such a road. Still, the possibility exists that one of us won't be able to continue on, and that road may be the only way out of here. Swallowing grimly at the thought, we finish our tea and move on.

The gateway to Manang Province is marked by an eight-foot-wide concrete post and lintel structure that spans the rocky trail. Against a faded red background, white Nepali letters dominate, but large vertical English letters down the right side clearly spell out a big "Welcome" to Western travelers. It is a clear recognition that our trekking dollars and love for this province enable it to survive.

From this point, the Marsyangdi River gorge widens into a flat gravelly plain, the river snaking through its bottom where the town of Tal sits at a vulnerable bow along one shallow bank.

Huge mountains intrude from both sides, promising to deliver rainfall and snow melt on a regular basis, but often in quantities that overwhelm. A steel trestle bridge spans the river at the narrow end, allowing supplies to arrive by road.

Regretting the loss of this one chance to cross a river where the bridge floor doesn't sway underfoot, I turn away from it with the others and follow the trail into town.

Chapter Eighteen

TAL TO DHARAPANI

Tal looks like a pretty frontier town, harkening back to the early days of the American West. We pass a row of stone buildings with flat roofs aligned next to a low stone wall. A young girl, about fourteen, squats beside the road weeding a patch of four-inch high corn and potato plants. On her back, she carries a baby about three months old held snug in a red woven sling. Round ears of a pink teddy bear outfit jut out from its fuzzy hood. Both seem content, but may also suffer from injustices common to frontier towns.

The girl could be simply caring for this child, but, in Nepal, odds are the baby is her own, conceived just after she reached puberty. If she's received any education at all, it's probably limited for her now, with only child-rearing and gardening left for her to do. In these remote regions, old customs die hard, and woman-friendly thinking has yet to take hold.

We find lunch in an outdoor courtyard situated a short distance from the dirt and dust of the street. Other hikers stroll by while we sip our tea. The weather, still mild at 5,500 feet, invites shedding of layers and the release of our feet from their prisons of leather. Still sweating inside heavy wool socks, my toes ache to be set free in the comfort of sandals. I'm ready to call it a day.

"Couldn't we sleep here tonight?" I say to Adam, knowing the answer even as I speak.

"No, Mom, we have to hike six hours today," he says, "We have a schedule to follow if we want to make it over the pass by the 15th."

Adam has mapped out our expedition day by day, unwilling at this point to give me any slack. Too many obstacles lie ahead to allow taking even half a day off. Better to push hard now while it's easy than to run short on time when the going gets rough.

Or is it that Adam actually enjoys making me suffer? I wouldn't be surprised, given the ordeals Adam endured during his childhood. Many times, we pushed him to hike with us when he was still small, his short legs having to move twice as fast as ours, just to keep up.

Even as he matured, hiking held little attraction for Adam. He'd rather play video games, or wage paint-ball battles with his friends, than hang out with Mom and Dad. The irony of him pushing us to hike farther now almost makes me want to laugh.

Almost, but not quite. Adam was young then, and his feet didn't hurt the way mine do now. He's also in denial about the fact that I'm older. One could say I asked for it. In any case, no sense complaining now that I'm here. Whining probably won't work for me now any more than it had worked for him then.

I turn my attention to what I'm eating, a dal bhat made delectable by the addition of mint to the spicy achar. The mint grew alongside the roadway on the way in, prompting me to make a quick association between it and what we're eating now.

Not all supplies come here on the backs of porters. Self-sufficiency is more the order of the day, and what we see growing or raised nearby will more than likely find its way into our food. I surmise our hot milk tea comes courtesy of the shaggy yak/cow hybrids contentedly grazing in the grassy meadow next door.

Before leaving Tal, we use the facilities, housed discreetly behind doors on the back wall of the courtyard. I'm pleased that the squat-johns are reasonably well maintained, and bar soap, so often absent, is provided for us.

Amita registers us as an official hiking group at a police checkpoint on the way out of town. We give her our TIMS cards and Trekking Permits, and with an obvious bearing of self-confidence, she passes them on to a man in a camouflage jacket and hat. He stares at us briefly, comparing photos and looking as official as his tin-roofed shelter will allow.

The officer could question Amita's credentials for acting as our guide, since she has no card to identify herself as such, but he doesn't; he simply records our names in his book, a new requirement for foreign travelers in Nepal. The process provides comfort to us that someone here is keeping track of our whereabouts. Should any of us need emergency services, part of the fee we paid will go toward our rescue.

It's not lost on me that passing Amita off as our guide is patently illegal, but, as we've seen, new laws in Nepal are not always followed. She's Nepali, so we've satisfied the basic intent, and if Adam is familiar with the trail we plan to follow, then we're covered as far as knowing the way we should go. Some hikers choose to venture into these mountains unguided, defying local laws altogether and putting their group and all potential rescuers at risk.

Steeper and rougher now, the trail cuts a crooked line along the canyon wall until a short suspension bridge leads us to the other side. Up ahead, we discover the reason for the bridge—a round pocket of bare rock scars the hillside where the trail had been. Below it, the river cuts around a massive boulder, which apparently fell from above, leaving behind not a shred of soil from which to rebuild the former trail.

Further up the gorge, and nestled near the bottom of a perfectly vertical rock face, a small-scale hydroelectric project is situated, demonstrating how Nepal takes advantage of this rugged terrain. Here gravity, ample water, and ingenuity have combined to provide a needed resource. Our next destination, Dharapani, lies just ahead. Thanks to this facility, it is replete with power and light.

Arriving in town, our group stops to read a sign painted on the side of the first guest house. It brags about their services:

Telephone Service * 24 hrs. cold and hot shower * Chinese, Nepali & Tibetan food * Laundry service * Available of porter & horses * Neat and Clean toilet bathroom on every floor * We cooking on gas * Camping place.

This venue is filled by a large group of hikers that booked ahead, so we're forced to choose other accommodations just down the road.

The proprietors of the place we choose also used to call Pokhara home. Since Amita is from there, the man and his wife easily fall into conversation with her. As they prepare our tea, Paul and Adam sit down to wait, and I clamber up the two flights of stairs separating me from my room.

The eight steps are steep and difficult to manage in my current state. A double mattress on the bed beckons, but I can't afford to give in. If I allow myself the luxury of lying down, I'll never get up, risking the loss of a precious commodity—hot water. Daylight and its associated heat is waning. If I wait too long to take a shower, the water will be too cold to tolerate.

Two small wooden buildings with concrete floors sit side-by-side in the back of the property. A white rope clothesline stretches between the small buildings and the buildings out front. A green rubber hose functions as shower head. I hold it aloft amid chilly air blowing through an open window.

Hordes of tiny goosebumps rise on my arms and legs as I scrub off the salty scum, happy I remembered soap, washcloth, and mini hiking towel.

My battered toes spread wide on the wet concrete, a dull soreness on the right side of my foot the only recognizable hint of my ailment. Against all odds, my feet survived the day and are doing fine. In fact, no new injuries cropped up during this first full day on the trail, and I have passed yet another test.

Upon our arrival, Adam had declared, "Now I know you're capable of hiking a 6-hour day."

"Great," I said, but held my resentment inside.

I could have worked up to it. It would have been better to hike four hours, followed by six, then eight. But, no, I had to prove myself yet again.

Somewhere there is a reason I keep signing up for trips like this, and subjecting myself to the inevitable trials. Pampering has never been part of Adam's style, nor was it his fathers before him. I wonder what drives me to push myself in this way.

Something tells me I must discover the answer for myself. It has something to do with not being left behind, or left out, but there's more to it than that. In another week, I will have finished this trek and know why I do this. By then, all of us will know whether taking this trek was a good idea.

Chapter Nineteen

DHARAPANI TO CHAME

After a good night's sleep, I awaken to use the squat-john, which, unfortunately, results in a plugged toilet. Amita, already awake and outside, has the whole (or hole) situation resolved before I know what to do, or anyone else is the wiser.

I didn't ask Amita to fix it. She just did, just as she's fixed everything for me since I arrived. It's like a knee-jerk reaction with her.

I know I must tell her I'm one who is not used to having things done for me, so it leaves me feeling a little uncomfortable. She may take offense, but if I do nothing, I'm taking advantage. Still, it's nice to have a helper, at least while I'm still in Nepal.

Our goal on this day is to reach Chame at 2,710 meters, or just under 9,000 feet. In an effort to make up the lost time, Paul and Adam stop a passing jeep driver just before breakfast. They try to negotiate a ride, but manage only to offend him with a ridiculously low offer. Lacking alternative options, we strap on our backpacks after breakfast and start walking on the jeep trail.

Just out of Dharapani, clear skies reveal Dhaulagiri Peak at nearly 27,000 feet, a solid white dome on the horizon. Together with the neighboring Annapurna range, they form the Marsyangdi Valley. Waterfalls from their generous snowpack regularly spill their contents into the Marsyangdi River.

Both peaks are also responsible for carving out the Kali Gandaki, the deepest river gorge anywhere on Earth. That gorge is on the east side of the circuit, where it's suspension bridges provided endless challenges for me seven years ago. I have yet to discover whether the bridges on this side will be as difficult to cross. Deeper gorges need only a short span to stretch across them, while wider gorges may require a much longer span.

In an effort to get a better shot of this landscape, Paul steps off the side of the road, nearly losing his balance and stumbling under the weight of his pack. Alarmed, Adam runs over to grab his shoulder, intent on stopping his fall.

"Damn it, Dad!" he says. "You can't afford to be careless around here. If you start rolling down any of these slopes, the weight of your pack will continue to pull you over and you won't be able to stop!"

The scene plays over again in my head as we continue up the road. I see Adam, in the present scolding his dad, but then drift back to a time when Adam was only two years old. We were walking on the Routeburn Track in New Zealand with Adam strapped firmly on my back. I put him down to stretch his legs while Paul and I stopped to catch our breath.

Paul cautioned Adam to stay on the trail, pointing out the steep drop-off on both sides, but Adam, so relieved to be free of his carrier, was having none of it. A few minutes later, we heard a loud shriek and turned to see our terrified little boy clinging to a root, his feet dangling in mid-air.

How long was it before we helped him? I don't remember, but Paul and I found amusement in our son's predicament. He hung only three inches from the ground and wasn't in any real danger, but since he couldn't see his feet, feared the distance was much farther.

The incident proved to be a perfect opportunity to teach Adam a lesson about minding his parents and paying attention to his footing on the trail. Having heard him scold his father just now, I know he learned his lesson well.

Three hours into the day, Paul and Adam grow nervous about the 16 miles still remaining between us and Chame. A first jeep with a load too full of riders has already passed, so they try flagging down another, just before we reach a 50-foot waterfall.

The waterfall holds me spellbound, not only by the height, but also by the fact that the jeep trail we're following passes right beneath its base. Any vehicle going that way must negotiate through a pool of water and over a narrow bridge of stones. I watch with trepidation as Adam and Paul talk to the driver.

Fortunately, Adam and Paul hold the same reservations I do about riding in a jeep under a waterfall. They arrange our ride to start on the other side, where the road markedly improves. The jeep crosses the narrow passage without us, and then waits at a wide bend in the road.

Behind the jeep, we walk through a fine spray of water from the volume that gushes from a huge fissure in the rock. A deep pool next to the roadbed now successfully drains through a large metal culvert, but this engenders no confidence that it will continue to do so during the upcoming monsoonal season. This is one more reason we might not want to return the same way we've come if we fail to complete the Annapurna Circuit.

For 1,500 rupees, the jeep driver agrees to take us to Chame along with his load of eggs. Amita and Adam climb into the front with the driver, while Paul and I share what's left of a back seat stacked high with cardboard boxes labeled "egg products." The Styrofoam cartons emit a squeaky sound as we begin rumbling up the road, and I hold my breath at each bump and jolt, trying to prevent the fragile cargo from breaking as my body presses against it.

Far from comfortable, the jeep offers only the time we saved by not walking this road. Just a few years ago, the road that we are riding on didn't exist, nor would the option to add a considerable delay, such as a wedding ceremony. I glimpse slivers of magnificent scenery compromised by my obstructed view from the back seat. We've lost something very precious in our haste to reach Chame, but the decision was necessary in order that we could share a beautiful wedding.

Chapter Twenty

HALF DAY IN CHAME

Our jeep arrives in Chame at about 2 p.m. with everything, including the eggs, more-or-less intact. Thanks to our motorized transport, we'll all get an extra half-day to rest. The driver parks in front of a collection of charming detached wooden chalets that sit in a sunny location to the rear of a restaurant and kitchen. Prominently displayed in front is a sign that reads "Free WIFI"—that seals the deal for Adam and Amita.

Having missed lunch on the way, we ditch our packs and sit down at long wooden tables inside. The room is brightly lit from a large picture window facing the street. Shelves full of bright silver bowls and platters line the walls. We request four orders of dal bhat and gleefully pull out our cell phones to check email.

Tracy, my childhood friend from Pennsylvania, has just sent a message inquiring what we're doing in Nepal. She lives in North Carolina now, and rarely has news of us unless she talks to my sister, who still lives in the area where we grew up. Word has spread across the miles, and I'm delighted to say hello and share our news.

As our young dark-haired male server sets down large metal plates of rice, greens, and turmeric-stained potatoes, I ask him to take a picture of us. We smile broadly over four plates still steaming hot. We're in a setting so remote that I could never have dreamed of being here when I was young, let alone transmitting a picture back to Tracy before our meal grows cold.

In the courtyard, in front of the chalets, a round stainless steel basin sits inside a deep rectangular sink; it is piled high with wet clothing. Since it's still early in the day, Amita and I dig out our dirty clothes, planning to wash those of our husbands and our own. I feel more Nepali here, struggling with the laundry, as if the task is assigned to me by gender alone. Amita seems to relish the chore, throwing her pile of laundry about as though it's a slab of meat she's tenderizing and about to cook.

I'm having my problems with it. The basin isn't big enough to contain both water and all the dirty laundry I want to wash. The sink drain is clogged and full of yucky soap-clouded water, unacceptable for soaking my dirty trail-worn clothes.

Once again, Amita intercedes. "Here," she says, "Let me show you how to wash clothes the Nepali way. Spread the clothing out on the drainboard of the sink and rub it with this little bar of soap. You can pile the clothes into the basin as you finish each piece. Then, when you're done applying the soap, just rinse the basin under the water tap and drain it over here. We'll use the wash water to make sure this garden grows well."

Behind me lies a previously unnoticed vegetable garden, where dozens of mustard greens grow tall in the afternoon sun, irrigated steadily by discarded wash water. Apparently, the reuse of water for different purposes isn't a novel idea in Nepal, and the proprietors of this establishment haven't failed to miss an opportunity for their patrons to participate. This technique works well, and it also ensures a plentiful supply of greens in our meals.

Our chalet sits behind the wash area, connected by a clothesline which extends between it and our tiny porch. Paul helps me hang clothes until we run out of clothespins and any space left on the line. I indiscreetly display our remaining socks and underwear around the perimeter of the porch.

Lying down separately on two single beds, we wait our turn for a solar shower. Several patrons use hot water before us, but as we close our eyes, the sun remains high in the sky.

The next thing I know, Paul is tugging at my foot, telling me it's time to get up. "Hurry," he says, "clouds have come in, and you might lose your chance for hot water."

I jump from my bed, the fog of sleep still upon me. Sandals and soap I had ready conspiratorially hide from me. Paul finds them, and pushes me out the door. I awaken further under a surprisingly hot shower.

After satisfying four healthy appetites in the restaurant around 5 p.m., we see Adam buying the deck of cards that had been on display in a case by the window.

"Want to play Texas Hold 'em?" he asks, eyebrow raised like a frontier gambler.

We respond in unison with an enthusiastic, "Yes!" and spend the evening learning the intricacies of this complicated game. Amita soaks up the information like a sponge, and since we don't have any poker chips, she serves as our official scorekeeper. She substitutes columns of numbers for imaginary chips, displaying impressive math skills. As the night wears on, we're left with a sense that, not only is Amita exceedingly helpful, she's also exceedingly bright.

That night I fall asleep thinking about my friend, Tracy, to whom I sent our picture earlier in the day. I remember us sitting together in the Pennsylvania cornfield that separated our two homes. We met there as eight-year-olds sharing saltine crackers slathered with summer softened butter and secrets held sacred in the quiet between corn rows. The memory of it makes me miss the company of women, so often absent from my world today.

Filling that role here in Nepal is Amita, potentially the daughter I never had. How much time I'll have with her after this trek is anyone's guess, but I'll make the best of the time I have now. I cherish every episode with her as though it were my very last.

Chapter Twenty-One

CHAME TO DHIKUR POKHARI

Wet socks! Not the greeting I'd hoped for as I emerge from our chalet. I'm barefoot, with hiking boots in hand, and all but my heaviest fleece on. The discovery that nearly eighteen hours wasn't nearly enough drying time for my heavy wool socks now threatens to derail our plans to get started early on our hike toward Lower Pisang. At 6:30 a.m., I stand in the doorway dangling my sopping socks as Adam and Amita emerge from their own chalet.

"They didn't dry," I say in a tone thick with exasperation, "and I washed both pairs. Now I don't have any socks to wear at all."

Adam responds with enthusiasm, "I have socks!" to which I release a burst of laughter.

"Are you gloating? I was expecting at least some sympathy."

"No, you don't understand. I've been looking for a way to justify all the extra socks I brought along— way more than I should have. Now you've given me a good reason to be carrying them."

"Okay then," I reply, still chuckling, "Glad I could help." My wet socks will be left to dangle from the outside of my pack until sunlight and warmer temperatures accomplish what nighttime temperatures could not.

Paul pushes past me, interrupting our mirthful episode. His gaze is fixed on the horizon, with both hands on our digital camera. He's on a mission to capture Lamjung Himal towering above us in all of its snowbound glory. We saw glimpses of it coming into town yesterday, but morning has delivered an unobstructed view; sun now reflects off its white surface, and frames it in striking cobalt blue. The 23,000-foot peak nearly blinds us with its brilliance.

Shivers and growling stomachs soon prevail, leading us inside the restaurant to steaming bowls of hot porridge. Email must also be checked one last time before tucking our cell phones safely away. The likelihood of finding connectivity beyond here is doubtful.

Evidence of the growing cold is on display again as we pass a local family on our way out of town. Next to a 20-foot wall of firewood, they squat atop a raised stone work area using hand tools for whittling and chopping their kindling. The man, looking about 50 years old, in a blue plaid shirt and denim trousers, sits cross-legged, knees flat to the ground. His round-faced wife in loose purple pajama pants and bright pink sweater squats competently beside him squarely on both of her feet. I recognize each of their postures, the tailor sit and common Hindu squat, as those of accomplished yoga practitioners, who make a living teaching chair-sitting seniors like me how to build strength and flexibility. Amita and Adam have already demonstrated they're still capable of such poses, and I expect they'll retain that flexibility for the rest of their lives. Having used these postures for several decades to combat my own back issues, I certainly hope they do.

Lower Pisang lies about eight miles away, and only 1,700 feet higher. We follow the road, along with just about everyone else, because it has replaced most sections of a former trail. The Marsyangdi River is on our left. Forests of pine and fir, interspersed with sections of a road blasted out of solid granite, afford the only horizontal walking surfaces for man or beast through here. At a narrow section of the road, we pass mules laden with loads of live chickens, forcing us to walk to the inside, dodging both their feathery cages and pieces of rock jutting out from the side of the road. Better here than on the outside, where the potential for being bumped over the edge presents a real and constant danger. Jeeps piled high with gear and top-riding passengers manage the same maneuvers as we do, while at the same time producing volumes of gray dust in their wake.

A cluster of stone and wood buildings provides a timely morning tea stop, after which the road leads us past a long *mani* wall. Two dozen 18-inch bronze-colored prayer wheels are set on a row of spindles, each about 18 inches tall. Each vertical cylinder is inscribed with the Buddhist mantra, *"Om Mani Padme Hum."* Above the prayer wheels, propped at various angles, is a collection of stone tablets, each carved with the same mantra. A Tibetan invention, prayer wheels are purported to provide benevolent blessings to all who spin them, view the stone tablets, or repeat the mantra contained inside.

I see this collection as a curiosity. It's hard to

believe good fortune can be so freely given, but neither am I prepared to pass them by unread or unspun. They may have played a part when we were last in Nepal. Good fortune smiled on us then, when any number of mishaps might have transpired. Like any good luck charm, they must at least offer a placebo effect.

Without questioning, Amita walks to the left of the wheels and starts spinning each one by pushing on its wooden base.

"They're meant to be spun clockwise," she says, so I follow her example, spinning them in the same way she does. As soon as mine have stopped, Paul starts the ones behind me spinning again, and Adam brings up the rear. By the time Amita has reached the end, we've got all of the wheels spinning at the same time, providing us with renewed assurance all will go well in the coming days.

Across the river gorge, a series of narrow waterfalls carve their way down the hillside, their base disappearing into a cinder and pine needle covered gray mound bordering the river. Closer inspection reveals the mound to be made of snow, the remnants of an avalanche that cascaded down the hillside the winter before. Recognizing this as the first snow on the trail, we're immediately mindful of what it portends. We'll be climbing above 10,000 feet before the day ends, where symptoms of altitude sickness may become an issue.

The sun beats down intensely as the day wears on, making shaded areas between rocky stretches of roadway preferred as cooler places to walk. We're led gradually into a broader, shade-filled valley, until one unmistakable feature rises above the evergreens to tower above us. A glacially carved edifice climbs nearly 5,000 feet in a smooth sweep upward into the clouds.

Paungda Danda, as it is known, literally translates to mean "Gateway to Heaven," and is revered locally as a mythical transport system for human souls headed for the afterlife. A crown of snow spreads majestically across its very top, imparting a feeling that souls making it this far will surely be given a peaceful rest.

Dwarfed by its presence for several more miles, we approach yet another suspension bridge. So long and narrow it must effectively end all travel by motorized transport, or so I think, until a single motorcyclist dashes that reasonable assumption. He simply zips across it, as though it presents no barrier to him at all.

After that exhibition, any objections I might have would seem shallow and weak. I swallow hard, holding my poles horizontally in one of my clinched fists and trudge determinedly across that bridge. The others wait on the other side.

Amita, apparently bored now by this routine, rests her poles horizontally across her shoulders and strolls casually across as if walking through a field of flowers. Not fazed by such trivialities as a suspension bridge, she's made of tougher stuff than that.

Were she anyone else, I'd probably be annoyed by Amita's casual, off-handed manner. She's definitely showing me up, but she doesn't seem to trivialize my fears. Instead, she pushes me past

Linda Schuyler Horning

them, providing the kind of example I need. If I spend enough time close to her, I might find the courage to do more than I otherwise would. This trek has become so much more rewarding for me now that Amita is part of our group.

154

Chapter Twenty-Two

DHIKUR POKHARI TO LOWER PISANG

At 1:00 p.m. we find our lunch stop at Dhikur Pokhari, where we share the backdrop of Paungda Danda with half a dozen lodges while enjoying our standard fare of dal bhat and "hot lemon."

Hot lemon, we've discovered, is a boiled drink with powdered lemon flavoring that comes out of a can. Real lemons need refrigeration and don't grow at high elevation, making this alternative to lemonade more practical for us, especially when everything we drink must be boiled. We linger while sipping it, taking the time to recuperate. Our goal for today lies only a few miles away over relatively flat terrain.

I check the condition of my feet, a little sore, but much better than expected considering the miles we've come. I'm beginning to sense something else may be at work here, presiding over the outcome of our expedition, and it fills me with new hope and optimism.

When Paul and I stand up ready to go, Adam seems reluctant to join us. I'm not sure if he's just tired, or needs some time alone with Amita. Either way, I figure he's entitled, and take him up on his suggestion that we start out alone.

The terrain widens into a bucolic, tree-filled valley inhabited by a few cattle grazing lazily on tender shoots of grass. One brown and white cow has recently dropped a calf, a perfect copy of herself in miniature, which she gently nuzzles with her light pink nose. Already, I find myself wishing Amita and Adam were here with us to see this, confident they'd be as taken as we are by the sweet tenderness embodied in this bovine pair.

Our separation today brings to mind a time in the past when Paul and I left toddler Adam alone. It was the first time we hired a sitter to care for him while taking a trip by ourselves.

We were living in Tasmania, Australia then, and thought a trip to Melbourne would give us both a break from childcare and diapering. We expected relief at finally being free to tour on our own.

Instead, we discovered that everywhere we went we realized how much we missed our son. He would have loved the Melbourne Zoo, and the tram ride getting there, and all the trucks and buses on the street. They just weren't the same without him.

Still without our traveling companions, Paul and I walk farther up the road, coming to a wide, flat river plain covered in stone cobbles. A wooden bridge crosses the Marsyangdi here; it rushes noisily through its channel, boiling continuously, and in the process, manufacturing new cobbles. This constant supply is used for bridge footings and channel stabilizers, as in the upcoming bridge. Cobbles encased neatly inside wire crib walls firmly support each end of a wooden span.

We walk confidently across the bridge until Paul stops suddenly, noticing a missing section of his hiking pole. It must have stuck in the cracks between planks in the bridge floor.

Searching for and failing to find it, I walk off the end of the bridge and peer into what looks like the bowels of a washing machine. Shaking my head, I think to myself, "not a chance," and return to the bridge empty-handed, only to see Paul sitting unconcerned under a tree on the other side.

Paul has picked up a stick and started whittling it into a round dowel. It will replace the missing end of his telescoping pole.

"Very resourceful!" I say with approval.

"We're not going to let a small thing like a broken hiking pole get in the way of progress," he replies, and with smug satisfaction, he presses the newly formed part onto the end of his pole.

"Perfect fit! This will do nicely."

Looking back in the direction of the bridge, we see Amita and Adam just coming into view. We're eager to tell them the story of the broken hiking pole, and to ask Amita if she saw the calf by the side of the road.

"Yes! I saw him." She responded. "He was so cute! I had to go over and pet him. The mother didn't seem to mind, and Adam took a picture of him while I had my arms around his neck."

"I knew you'd love seeing him!" I told her with a hug, "But I was afraid he and his mother might move away from the trail before you had your chance."

Silently, I mourn the loss of a shared episode, realizing how selfish I've become. It's a trait I've picked up as I grow old, knowing the days ahead of me are fewer than those behind. It frightens me to think about how much more I'll miss before my time runs out.

We walk together to Lower Pisang, booking the first place we see on the lower edge of town. Two freshly-built, long wooden barracks sit at right angles to each other with an attached wooden porch on one side. We arrive in time to take cold showers and wash clothes, hanging them neatly on a line strung under wide porch eaves designed for that purpose.

The last rays of sun over snowy Annapurna II make us wish we had time for a day hike to Upper Pisang. Its Buddhist temple and stunning mountain views, barely visible from our lodge, tempt many younger hikers who have higher energy levels than we do.

Our group chooses to stay at our new establishment, eating a late dinner in the restaurant. Here, charcoal heaters placed under long wooden tables keep us warm while we linger playing Texas Hold 'em. Night falls slowly outside the window.

An American man, about middle-aged, sits behind us talking to another hiker about his decision to turn back. He and his young Asian wife failed to hike as far as they'd planned. She had been getting headaches and feeling nauseous, both convincing them these symptoms were too severe. They'd gotten as far as Manang, our next port of call.

Adam turns around to address them both, "You

could have stayed another night. It would have given you both more time to acclimatize."

Dismissing Adam, his wife replies, "I just felt awful. I needed to go down."

Adam shrugs and says no more, returning to the plate in front of him, but later, after the couple leaves, he confides in us what he really thinks.

"They didn't even stay another night," he complains, as if their decision to turn back had been a huge blunder.

Paul replies, "I respect their decision. You never know when altitude sickness is going to strike. People respond in different ways."

"Yes, but you've got to give it enough time!" he growls. "She could have taken Diamox." Shaking his head sadly, he continues, "She just gave up too soon."

Paul lets the matter drop, choosing not to further inflame his irritated son, but later he brings it up with me when we're alone in our room.

"Adam showed no sympathy to that American couple at all," he said. "It makes me think we're headed for trouble if any of us develop problems."

"You're right," I say. "He seems to think going over the pass is a foregone conclusion, when any number of things could go wrong for us between now and that day. I guess he's as stubborn as he's always been. That's just fine when it only concerns him, but there are three other people here. He'd better start showing some compassion, or we're all headed for trouble."

Privately, however, I realize not all of my thoughts are so negative. I'm buoyed by my own body's response to the challenges so far, and I've begun to think going over the pass is possible. My optimism stems in part from an irrational faith in the powers of the region, with its prayer wheels, prayer flags and holy places. I sense a magical element protecting us. There is no other reasonable explanation.

It's dangerous to put too much faith in magic, but people here do amazing things—like riding motorcycles over suspension bridges and living to talk about it. Their faith may be carrying them through, not just excessive confidence or bravado. Amita's way ahead of us in this respect. She knows what faith can do, and seems comfortable with all of it.

She's also comfortable with us, which is an amazing thing, considering the difference in our backgrounds. The subtle bonding taking place here might be what she planned all along. She'll know us at the end of this trip more intimately than most new brides come to know their in-laws over a lifetime, but whether she remembers us fondly or not may depend on what happens in the coming days.

Chapter Twenty-Three

LOWER PISANG TO HUMDE

After four days, a cohesive camaraderie replaces the awkwardness that permeated the beginning of our trek. We pack and eat at first light, starting out at 7:30 a.m., our earliest time yet. The top of Paul's ears, thoroughly fried by three days of too much sun, now find themselves shielded by the brim of Amita's pink straw hat.

It's an eccentric look, but practical. Paul recognized his need to take protective measures about the same time Amita tired of carrying her hat. She wears a scarf most of the time, anyway, and is happy to be relieved of her burden. In addition, a chemical peel Paul endured two years ago convinced him he isn't invincible when it comes to the sun. The minor embarrassment he suffers now by wearing Amita's pink hat pales by comparison to the prospect of addressing a new issue later with his dermatologist.

As we pass through the rest of Lower Pisang on our way out of town, we discover how much more it had to offer if we'd taken the time to look around the night before. Multiple eating establishments and guest houses line the street, and another mani wall of prayer wheels, artfully draped with several ropes of faded and tattered prayer flags, occupies its center.

The mani wall calls to us, demanding that we do our work to attract more blessings. Dutifully, we line up in concert, walking in a clockwise direction around them like a seasoned and devoted band of followers.

Unlike the rocky terrain that dominated the first part of this trail, the road we follow now is carved through a wooded landscape that allows for the formation of soil. Our footsteps are quieter, but the sound of breathing becomes more dominant, as frequent rest breaks begin to punctuate our climb. We take them spontaneously now, as the high altitude begins to take its toll. Switchbacks in the road offer opportunities for shortcuts through the woods, but also present additional obstacles to climb up or go around.

Pausing at one, I exclaim, "You've got to be kidding!" Then I climb twenty feet, straight up, around a boulder. A young male hiker ahead of me offers a hand, and I take it, grateful for this one chance to spare my knees.

Overall, I'm proud of how well I'm holding up. As each challenge adds new burdens to my legs and knees, they respond appropriately, growing stronger day by day. Both have been bound in pharmacy grade elastic knee braces from the start, a precaution held over from our trek of seven years ago. They may no longer be necessary, but I'm not willing to take the chance. Most of the time they don't show under my loose-fitting zip-off pants, but I don't care if they spoil my image.

Walking alongside other hikers, our group does create a curious look—I in my knee braces and Paul in his pink straw hat; Adam and Amita, so obviously a couple, but seriously different in terms of complexion and height. Each one of us is enough to make anyone smile.

Adam frequently offers Amita help, adjusting her backpack, and sharing a common water bottle. He calls her "*Budi*," which means "wife" in Nepali, and holds her hand or caresses her shoulder from time to time. Paul and I derive parental pleasure from witnessing each gesture, as it reinforces our belief that they are in love.

Resting at a roadside bench, we're approached by a Polish woman who introduces herself. We're happy to share our story and tell her about our plans. She takes our picture and we chat for a while, feeling good about her mostly favorable remarks. As she turns to go, however, she spoils it all with parting words that leave us feeling less than flattered.

"You're very lucky to be able to hike this well," she says. "Most old folks can't do this sort of thing."

The condescension in her words stings Paul and I in a way we can't explain. Had we been thinking we weren't old, by virtue of the fact we've made it this far? Clearly, the release of our vanity has only gone so far, and we don't like being forced to admit to the obvious. As we continue, we'll do our best to prove "old" is only a relative term.

At the top of a rise, we pause to admire the view of Humde Valley. Like the mark of a branding iron, the Humde Airport scars the center of a flat-bottomed bowl, allowing shade only around the edges where the trail winds its way generously through the woods. We'll easily reach the town of Humde by lunchtime over relatively flat and downhill terrain.

After what feels like an easy stroll, we come into town, ordering our standard fare from a restaurant perched on a second-floor wooden balcony. Steep, narrow steps take us up to a bird's eye view of the town square, where mules now share the road with everyone else. Beyond this point, passable roads don't exist to serve the motorized competition, so the usefulness of these four-legged creatures is clearly established. Brightly-colored tassels on their harnesses and saddles clearly celebrate their right to be here.

While waiting for lunch to be served, it seems reasonable to find the closest toilet facility and take care of business before it's time to move on. I find it in a room behind us in the rear of the building, quite private and unusually convenient. The ceramic squat-john nestles comfortably in a raised base of concrete with a nearby window offering light from outside. A red plastic bucket holds water for cleaning one's derrière, with a water tap hovering above it ready to refill. Also displayed is a bottle of Lysol Toilet Bowl Cleaner, undeniable evidence of its exemplary standard of cleanliness. I step inside and close the door.

Returning to the eating area, I stow my sealed

container of baby wipes discreetly back where it belongs, only to have Paul thrust his smelly socked foot in my direction. Without any perceptible sense of decorum, he yawns and stretches, addressing me in a casual way.

"You might want to kick off your boots and stay a while."

My husband enjoys this single aspect of our trek as much as any other. The total absence of propriety makes it all worth it in his eyes. He actually relishes the opportunity to behave as though he lives in a barn.

I take a seat beside my husband on the wooden step, ignoring his brutish ways. I'm less enthusiastic about behaving without decorum, but I realize it's a little late for me to fuss about such things. Beyond here, there's no telling what kind of facilities we'll find, whether we like it or not. We will need to accept conditions as we find them. It's nice to know, however, the proprietors here have done their best to make sure their place is clean for visitors. I am grateful we have a nice place to sit in the shade.

After our drinks are delivered, we spend the better part of an hour pondering such thoughts, while we rest our legs and drink tea.

Chapter Twenty-Four

HUMDE TO MANANG

Adam jumps up, checking his phone for the time, after which he urgently addresses us, "We have to get to Manang by 3:00 p.m. or we'll miss the lecture."

He wants us to hear a talk provided by the Himalayan Rescue Association (HRA), whose purpose is to educate climbers about the dangers of altitude sickness. His dad seems unimpressed, prompting Adam to persist with more intensity.

"It's really a good lecture, and I think it's important that you hear it."

"OK, OK. We'll do our best," responds Paul idly, "but if our dahl bhat doesn't get here pretty soon, it will already be too late to get there on time."

When the meal arrives, our boots are retied and we're ready to go. For a change, we don't linger, passing on the second portions we usually wolf down. Rising almost in unison, we put on our packs, and proceed immediately to an outdoor desk to pay the bill.

A phalanx of prayer wheels and teams of decorated mules dominate the street as we head out of town. Like veteran trekkers, we mix with the milieu, making sure good karma accumulates with us as it's meant to.

The trail to Manang leads us over relatively flat dry terrain that turns increasingly pale in color as the pine forest shrinks and dwindles to nothing. Snow-capped peaks line dry ridges in every direction, as a shrunken foreground amplifies grand landscapes rising ahead.

The Marsyangdi River stays with us, occupying our landscape to the right for the first several miles. She grows ever more clouded from finely ground rock known as "glacial flour," until turning powder blue as we look down on her from an aluminum trestle bridge. Leading us onward, the river flows from our high-altitude destination, becoming more real with each step that we take.

Though we're gaining only a few hundred feet more of elevation, we're now well above 10,000 feet. Adam campaigns harder to make sure we all drink plenty of water, asking each of us to drink at least two liters of water before reaching Manang. Adam has learned high urine output is a sign our bodies are adjusting to the higher altitude, helping our kidneys in particular to respond to the added stress.

With Adam's request comes a new inconvenience. More drinking inevitably leads to more frequent stops to relieve ourselves, each one slowing us and compromising our ability to reach Manang in the time we've allowed. As we approach the picturesque stone buildings and stupas of Manang, my watch shows we're just minutes after our planned arrival time.

In prehistoric times, stupas were simply dome-shaped mounds of earth where important kings were buried. Now, these ancient Buddhist shrines are more decorative and colorful, honoring the living, while they celebrate the awakened state of mind. Stupas decorate the base of a green terraced hillside just below where snow-capped mountains rise from the valley floor.

Forestalling our admiration of their beauty, we pass quickly by a large stupa on our way through the city gate. We are in a hurry to our secondary destination, the Himalayan Rescue Association's presentation.

As we arrive, a white wooden door in the stone pavilion is closed. We slip silently inside, just as the presentation starts to wind down. Many of those attending still linger, taking advantage of medical services available in the rear. For 100 rupees each (or approximately 10 cents American), we can measure our heart rate and the oxygen saturation level in our blood.

We stand in line briefly with other hikers, handing over the required currency. The reading is taken from a clip-type sensor placed on our index finger. Results show we're all within normal range. We're surprised, but the readings also reveal who among us seems to be most fit:

1. Adam: HR 78, O2 Sat 94
2. Paul: HR 62, O2 Sat 94
3. Me: HR 85, O2 Sat 92
4. Amita: HR 100, O2 Sat 91

Adam studies the figures, rubbing his chin, and finally addressing his dad. "You have the lowest pulse rate, and actually match my oxygen saturation level. This news bodes well for us in terms of the chances we'll do well at a higher elevation, but I can't help feeling a little disappointed. I'm half your age. Why don't I have the best result?"

Paul responds with a palms-up shoulder shrug and sheepish grin. "What can I say? I guess I just got what it takes." But Paul's lingering grin tells us more about what this result does for his ego. He's more than happy he had this chance to get the best of his son.

Choosing which hotel to stay in for the next two days occupies much of our afternoon. It's a task beset with several problems. For instance, Paul and I are happy with the solar showers and en-suite rooms at the first hotel, but the proprietor there refuses to comp Amita's meals without proof she's a certified trekking guide. We're reluctant to split up, but Amita and Adam take offense over what they consider to be rude behavior, and decide to take their business somewhere else.

They choose a hotel complex where rooms are decidedly more spare, but the restaurant is among the best in town. The dining room is spacious, rustic-looking, and sports a large copper pot which sits on a wood-burning stove in the center. This place has good food, and sees no problem with providing Amita's meals there for free, as our trekking guide.

Having settled the issue of where to sleep, we huddle together again to decide our next course of action. Manang has a lot to offer, as isolated as the town might seem at first glance. Many longer treks resupply here before climbing the higher reaches beyond. It's the last real chance to buy clothing before hiking over the pass.

Most of the buildings in Manang are made of stone and reach two or three stories high. A stone sidewalk covers the dirt street on the left side, but a sidewalk is not provided on the right side, where for a short time, a small grassy paddock can be enjoyed behind a wooden fence. In the rear of the paddock, a wooden sign advertises potable drinking water for sale. The door is closed as we approach, and no one is around to offer help. Somewhat dejected, we turn away, planning another visit later when we can fill all of our water bladders and bottles at once.

Several small stores and shopping stalls lie scattered about town. I'm concerned my nylon hiking pants won't be warm enough beyond here without an added thermal liner. Several stalls offer brightly colored tights, but they're too small, sized to fit a tall Nepali, but not a mature Western woman like me.

Only one small storefront offers a solution, but it's less than attractive. Wrapped in cellophane and off to one side are a drab pair of grannie-style thermals. Oh, the horror! But I know they'll be perfect for the job. I choose those, as well as a pair of red nylon gloves for me and an extra pair of mittens for Paul. Rain and light snow fall as we leave the shop.

Returning to our rooms, Paul and I enjoy our coveted hot-water shower. It's not that fancy, made of concrete with a bit of tile around the shower; a white porcelain squat-john sits in a raised platform next to the window, offering a spectacular view of *Annapurna IV*. We have it all to ourselves, negating the need for a trip down the hall in the middle of the night.

I dry my hair while enjoying the company of Adam, Amita, and other hikers in the dining room of their hotel. The food is good, the portions generous, and the wood stove offers warmth against the growing cold. We linger long after dinner, playing Texas Hold 'em and absorbing the ambiance of an old Himalayan hotel.

At last growing tired, Paul and I walk the 50 yards back up the stone-covered street to our hotel. Our room is set up with two separate beds, which Paul and I decide to keep apart. This is a change for us, but we want to maximize our chances of getting a good night's sleep. Paul always sleeps hotter than I do, so we won't fight over how much bedding to use, and we won't disturb each other if we get up in the night. I turn out the light, hopeful that we'll both sleep well.

ॐ

Chapter Twenty-Five

REST DAY IN MANANG

I sleep well that first night in Manang, but Paul's night is plagued with disruptions. He wakes feeling exhausted. By the time we meet Amita and Adam for breakfast, his queasy stomach exacerbates an already impatient and grumpy mood.

"How did you sleep?" chirps Amita, eyes bright and black hair shining after her morning shower.

"Not well at all," Paul grumbles, his voice low and groggy. "I'm glad we're staying here another night to acclimatize. I need at least one good night of sleep before I can think of climbing higher."

"We'll take a local hike today," offers Adam. "That should tire you out and allow for a nap in the afternoon before we go back to hear the full HRA presentation. Then, if you need some drugs to help you sleep, you can get a recommendation there from the doctors."

Just as we finish our breakfast, the proprietor of the hotel where Paul and I are staying shows up in our restaurant and calls Paul aside. He tells Paul that we need to pay an additional 1,000 rupees because we didn't take our meals in his establishment.

I watch with trepidation as Paul's body language

stiffens and he prepares to respond. This man hasn't chosen an opportune time to approach my husband. Predictably, Paul shows little compassion or sympathy toward the man or his complaint.

"This was not part of our deal," he says. "I made no promises I'd be taking my meals there, and I don't owe you any money."

The man makes a few more attempts, without success, to convince Paul that it was his error, but in the end Paul does agree we'll take our next two meals in his establishment. This seems to placate the man, since he turns abruptly and walks out. Paul seems satisfied, but has yet to learn the consequences of his decision, which we will both suffer later on.

For now, the day hike offers a chance for Paul to calm his temper and the rest of us to enjoy extraordinary scenery outside. Just across the river valley from Manang village sits a milky blue glacial lake fed by the waters of Gangapurna and Annapurna III peaks. A faint trail winds its way along the side of a bare dirt moraine that serves as a dam holding the high lake in place. While beautiful to look at and photograph, a climb in that direction seems too demanding for any of us to try today.

Instead, we turn west toward the Marsyangdi River, dipping low to the river plain, and then we loop back up again to a height of almost 12,000 feet. From this height, we can see all of Manang *Valley*, with snow-capped Annapurna II still shining to the west, and to the south, the impressive Gangapurna Glacier hanging impressively below Annapurna III.

Unencumbered by backpacks, we find our day

hike exhilarating, and hope it will offer therapeutic benefits to us, as well. In terms of acclimatization, hiking high and sleeping low helps our bodies to form new red blood cells, which are capable of carrying more oxygen. Theoretically, we can gain as much as 1,000 feet in a single day, so long as we sleep lower than the altitude to which we climbed. Tomorrow, with heightened blood oxygen saturation levels, we should be able to climb even higher.

While we struggle with our limitations, those who live in the village seem less affected. Among similar populations around the world, the people here have bodies that are known to have permanently adapted to living and working at elevations above 10,000 feet.

In addition, though they may live in primitive stone buildings, their use of cell phones and satellite dishes, prevalent on each of their rooftops, puts them far ahead of other third-world countries who stay less informed about technology. As we pass by the walls of their courtyards on our way back through the west side of Manang, our nostrils fill with the pungent aroma of burning cedar boughs, still smoldering in brass bowls from morning rituals. At least the offerings, I reason, serve as evidence they haven't lost all their ancient customs and traditions.

We split up for lunch as planned, Paul and I going to our hotel to take showers and lie down before a planned 3 p.m. rendezvous. We've plenty of time, but Paul still doesn't sleep. Now seriously concerned, he returns to the clinic with us in time to hear the full HRA presentation and speak with a doctor.

The room is nearly full of hikers when the lecture begins. On a flip chart at the front of the room is a list of all types of Acute Mountain Sickness (AMS). A digital projector stands at the ready. Our presenter is one of two doctors, and he begins the discussion by introducing himself and explaining the different terms.

"Acute Mountain Sickness," he says, "consists of a headache plus any one of the following symptoms to different degrees: nausea, tiredness, sleeplessness or dizziness, occurring at altitudes of around 8,000 feet or higher where patho-physiological changes due to lack of oxygen may manifest."

I look at Paul and shift uncomfortably in my seat. Adam leans over and whispers in my ear, "Dad hasn't had a headache, and he has the best blood oxygen levels any of us do."

"Two life-threatening complications," he goes on to say, "are water accumulation in the brain (high altitude cerebral edema, HACE) or high altitude pulmonary edema (HAPE, water accumulation in the lungs). The latter two complications may follow AMS, especially when people continue to ascend in the face of increasing symptoms. Those most in danger from complications are people who do not 'listen to their body', and heed the early warning signals of AMS; they can go on to suffer from HAPE and HACE and may even die."

The American doctor, one of many first-year physicians who take this assignment in order to combine hiking, living in a foreign country, and gaining valuable work experience, stays on to answer any questions. After speaking with Paul, he suggests that he take a drug called acetazolamide, better known as Diamox. Among other things, it is said to increase breathing rate, and therefore acclimatization. He also mentions Ambien as the only sleep aid that won't interfere with that process.

Sufficiently chastened against the dangers we face, but fortified with new knowledge, we return to our favorite restaurant to drink tea and take drugs. Adam happens to have a small stock of Diamox in his backpack, so we choose it to initiate our defensive program. The dose recommended by the doctor requires two pills, and Paul isn't sure how he'll react, so he decides to take only one. Amita, although not burdened specifically with any symptom, decides to take the other. Adam and I don't take anything, drinking only hot lemon tea. We part again to have dinner separately at our respective hotels.

The room Paul and I stay in is located on the third floor, so getting to the restaurant requires only that we descend down one flight of stairs. Behind a heavy wooden door lies the main restaurant with multiple tables and straight-backed chairs. We choose to explore a cozier rear section populated by padded benches and a pot-belly stove.

Groups of fellow hikers nestle in various corners, or sit warming themselves by the stove. A chalk board hangs by the door announcing yak chili as the evening's special. Picturing chili con carne made with yak meat, I choose that for myself, and Paul orders a vegetable and rice dish we think will make a nice accompaniment. As is often the case, we plan to share the two meals between us.

After a considerable wait, the dish arrives, and I can't help showing my disappointment. Apparently, chili con carne is unknown here, but hot peppers from whence it gets its name are well established. The dish contains only thin strips of dry-looking meat, garnished generously with dark red chili peppers. The meat is tough and too spicy for us, but we do our best to finish it, since the other dish isn't enough to sustain us both by itself. We leave feeling less than satisfied, and with an ominous burning sensation in both our stomachs.

Chapter Twenty-Six

MOMENT OF TRUTH

The night is painfully long and offers little sleep. Between heartburn from the yak chili and Paul's hyperventilation from the effects of Diamox, the night is not only without sleep, it's fraught with a unique element of terror.

The effects of altitude sickness can be subtle, difficult to sort out, and impossible to quantify. Sleeplessness is one symptom, but shortness of breath and headaches are relative conditions. It's kind of like trying to identify mild symptoms of heart attack without the aid of modern medicine.

We sit up at first light to compare notes.

"I can't go on," says Paul. "This makes two nights and days I haven't slept at all, and that Diamox was a big mistake."

Shifting my position on the bed, I take some time to respond. This isn't the outcome I'd hoped for.

"Adam will be heartbroken," I say, trying not to take sides on who is right or wrong, but it surprises me Paul wants to turn back, and not me.

All along I thought I was the weakest link. Paul, by far the stronger of we two, incessantly badgers me to push on. Now he plans to quash the expedition, and I'm not sure it's the right thing to do.

"That may be true, but he doesn't give a rat's ass about me. He's just focused on getting over the pass at any cost. Never mind the fact that I haven't slept for two days."

I'm sympathetic but also disappointed, and I wonder if Paul is giving it a fair shot. Could he be testing the rest of us to see if we'll comply, or is he testing his son's will against his own?

But this isn't about who's in charge, or who is not. It's about the strength of our unit as a whole. If we don't work together to solve this issue, all our hard-won camaraderie will be lost. I'm afraid of what will happen when we tell Adam the bad news. He's already shown how unsympathetic he is to those who've turned around. This outcome might be an impossible one for him to accept.

We pack our bags with heavy hearts, and prepare to move out of our hotel, but, true to our word, we eat breakfast here before moving on to to tell Adam and Amita the bad news. Both Adam and Amita listen quietly, as if they've already guessed what we'd say. But, instead of immediately acquiescing, Adam says, "Wait until 9 a.m. when the clinic opens. That way you can talk to the doctors one last time before you decide."

Too tired to argue, Paul replies, "All right, but I need to lie down again while I wait. I'm going back to our hotel to rest."

Adam, Amita, and I are left to weigh our options alone. We walk around town refilling water bottles at the potable water station, drinking tea and eating the offerings at a local bakery. Adam seems unable to accept possible defeat, and focuses instead on taking us over the pass.

"We still can do this," he enthuses. "One more day in Manang won't slow us down too much. We still have time to get you back to Kathmandu in time to make your flight home."

"I'm not sure Paul can make it, Adam," I say. "I know what it's like to go without sleep. It's no fun. Add to that the demands of climbing at this elevation, and he could start having problems with his heart. In that case, what would we do? We're playing a dangerous game."

Amita, wanting to support us both, chimes in, "Let's wait to see what the doctor says. Maybe he'll convince him to stay another night."

Promptly at 9 a.m., I go up to our room to wake Paul. Finding him gone, I rush back to Adam and Amita, where together we leave to chase him down at the clinic. We find him meeting with the other doctor, a female MD, who graciously allows me to join them in the consultation room.

"Take zolpidem," she advises, "and it will help you sleep, but you'll need to go down in elevation to relieve more of your symptoms."

We finish our meeting with her, taking her prescription and going outside where the doctor we initially spoke with sits relaxing in the sunshine with Adam and Amita. What he said to them gives renewed hope to Adam and raises doubts about what we'll be doing today.

"I think it's a bad idea to take more

acetazolamide." he says, "It obviously doesn't agree with you. The major culprit here is lack of sleep, not elevation sickness. If you get that taken care of, you'll be good to go."

In his present state, Paul is not impressed, so he beckons me to return to our hotel with him to pick up our bags and check out. Afterward, we return to our now-familiar restaurant to sit and wait for Adam and Amita.

They show briefly to deliver this news: "We've been pricing out motorcycles, and we can hire them to take us down the mountain. We'll ride on the back, as passengers."

The thought is enough to send shivers up my spine. Paul and I exchange a glance, each of us knowing a bouncy ride on a motorcycle would be more than either of our aging backs could tolerate. And the bridges, oh my gosh! Briefly imagining myself flying across a suspension bridge on the back of one of those mechanical beasts, my head begins to swing violently left and right.

Uttering an emphatic "No!" I lay my head down on my folded arms on the table in front of me.

Adam gets the message. They leave disappointed, but, we believe, resigned to our fate.

We sit drinking tea again, waiting more than an hour while a fierce wind whips up outside, making all thoughts of heading down the mountain today progressively less wise. The last terrain we'd covered before Manang had been relatively flat, leaving fewer opportunities for elevation loss until traveling much farther down. With the few hours remaining in the day, we'd only be able to drop about 500 feet before looking for new lodging for the night. That wouldn't be enough to relieve Paul's altitude sickness, and would only serve to tire him out more than he already is.

"We'll probably have to stay in Manang another night," Paul finally concedes. "Would you mind finding Adam and Amita to learn why they haven't come down? I'm too tired to do anything else right now."

Chapter Twenty-Seven

HIS CHAMPION

The rooms where Adam and Amita stay branch out on either side of a long wooden hallway. A bare light bulb and tall window at the end illuminate the way. I find them near the end of the hallway beyond an open door. Adam and Amita stand between two single beds, their packs sitting on them mostly full. I feel the sadness in the room as I walk inside.

"Paul doesn't want to go down from here anymore than you do, Adam. He just can't sleep," I say. "I'm sorry it's not turning out the way you wanted."

Turning to me with tears in his eyes, he pleads, "I just wanted him to try one more night."

That did it. My two arms reach out, encircling his waist, while his chin rests on the top of my head. Sobbing ensues, while Amita wraps her arms around both of us, forming a love huddle out of which no one wants to break free. I back off first to speak.

Wiping my eyes, I say, "I think your father can be convinced to stay another night. A wind has come up, and we probably wouldn't lose enough elevation to make a difference in his condition today, anyway."

"Oh, do you think so?"

"Yes. Why don't you go down and speak to him right now? You can leave your pack here."

As Adam runs past me, I feel only a little guilty for taking the credit for this. If I were honest, I should have said he'd already decided to stay in Manang, but the temptation to be his champion is too much to pass up. My adult son doesn't come to me anymore for support, and I miss it.

Amita and I talk a while before rejoining the guys in the restaurant. She tries to stay neutral, as I do, but it pains us to see our two men so terribly at odds.

"Both men are stubborn mules," I say. "Whether to stay or go has become almost a contest of wills."

"I worry the affection they have for each other could suffer before this expedition is through," Amita adds. "Let's agree to remind them not to lose sight of what is important here."

As we'd hoped, Paul and Adam talk easily as we enter the restaurant. They're getting ready to order lunch. Paul has already checked, and the room next to Adam and Amita is available to rent.

After lunch, we move in, and Adam digs out his Kindle for Paul. He thinks some reading might help to bring on sleep, and it turns out he's right. I pull out a book I've brought along and both of us nod off easily afterward to sleep for a full hour.

With everyone feeling refreshed, we take an easy stroll around town together peeking into shops and buying little treats to put into our packs. Adam is fond of yak cheese, so we enter a small storefront where the shopkeeper cuts off a chunk and weighs it on a balance scale, then wraps it in wax paper and ties it with string. It will come in handy, whether we climb higher or not.

Nearby, a larger storefront advertises an impressive inventory of clothing. We walk inside and browse the shelves for anything we might need. I see a purple cotton scarf printed with a drawing of the Annapurna Circuit that might be useful against the cold. Scooping it up, I recognize its value as a souvenir, but secretly wish our original plans hadn't changed. If we don't finish the Circuit, I can't wear it back in California as evidence we reached our goal.

That night, after multiple games of Texas Hold 'em in the restaurant, Paul and I reflect on people we've known through the years who loved to hike. Two died just recently, but had been able to amble through their favorite mountains right until the end, one even being found by fellow hikers on the trail after he'd passed.

"That's the way I want to go," declares Paul. "I want none of having a disabling condition first that prevents you from getting out on the trail."

"Then you should be willing to go over the pass," Adam tells Paul. They exchange looks, but Paul has no answer for him.

I respond to Adam by saying, "You'll never forgive yourself if anything happens to your father."

When we return to our side-by-side rooms to sleep, Paul finally takes the Ambien, and, as an extra precaution, a dose of Imodium, as well, this last to address a new issue that cropped up with his stomach after our evening meal. I'm beginning to feel like a walking pharmacy as we prepare to go over the Thorong La Pass.

The information from the HRA lecture listed upset stomachs right up there with sleeplessness as a sign of high altitude sickness. Since my stomach is fine, I doubt Paul's problem has anything to do with the food. Paul picks up the Kindle to read, and I lie awake wondering what tomorrow will bring.

As it stands now, we're planning to head back, each step in that direction admitting defeat. *It doesn't matter*, I tell myself. *We knew the risks, the odds of all four of us being able to pull it off. Wasn't the chance to be together enough? Isn't our health more important than completing this Circuit?*

Those thoughts ring hollow compared to a slim chance all will be right by morning. Trying to be neutral, sensible, and practical doesn't work for me. Just like my 34-year-old son, I am desperate to go over the pass.

Chapter Twenty-Eight

MANANG TO THE TEA STOP

We climb out of Manang Valley together, a renewed sense of purpose driving each step, for what had been a major crisis the night before now seems resolved. Paul arrived at breakfast feeling much better, with energy enough to give our quest another try.

"I'm ready to climb at least 1,500 feet to the next town," he announced, "and, if the Ambien continues to work, I'll keep on going after that. The doctor who believed it was lack of sleep and not altitude sickness causing my problem was probably right."

Ecstatic at hearing this announcement, Adam's face sprouted a huge grin, which he immediately tried to suppress. The effort didn't work very well. Adam's dimples grew in size even as he clamped his lips shut. It wasn't an 'I told you so', smile, just a happy one. Getting his dad back on board with him was all he'd been hoping for.

Amita and I exchanged giddy smiles of our own.

Our personal ambitions, less strong than those of the men from the start, grew with the change in elevation. We, too, could see ourselves ahead in the clouds. We tried to remain neutral through all of this, but now were breathing a sigh of relief. With so much of ourselves invested, we were anxious to have our own chance to make it over the pass.

The high mountain air was bitingly cold when we started this morning. We wore fleece shirts and pullovers, but then quickly shed them as the sun rose. Now we favor brightly colored nylon windbreakers and sun hats, a garb more appropriate for the superb weather we've drawn today.

When I notice it, I'm incredulous—not new pain or soreness, but a lack thereof. The tenderness under the ball of my right foot, a cause of constant concern in the days leading up to this, is now totally absent. The pain should be worse by now, but it's not. It doesn't exist. *How is that possible?* Looking down, I check to see if the feet beneath me are the same ones on which I started. They are.

"Paul," I breathe so only he can hear, "I don't feel my neuroma! I mean, it's as if I don't have it any more. My foot feels absolutely normal."

Paul responds without breaking his stride, "That's great! We thought it might be causing you a lot of trouble by now, but you say it's getting better? That makes two things we can celebrate! This is turning out to be a really good day after all."

Snow-capped peaks flank us on all sides, some fanning out into vast rockbound snowfields, others jutting majestically toward the sky. They're the same mountains we saw while in Manang, but they look larger now, viewed from a higher angle, to the north. The Annapurna massif, demarcated by Annapurna II, III, IV, and Gangapurna, represent a huge section of the planet's crust gradually being lifted by the collision of two or more tectonic plates. Here it displays itself before us, as a gigantic ridge of rock sparkling against a cloudless blue sky.

Yak Kharka, our next destination at 13,500 feet is named for the high mountain meadows that offer pasture for grazing animals. We spot our first goat from far off and wonder if there'll be more; then rounding the next bend we find ourselves walking beside a large herd.

Fascinated, we shed our packs, stopping to have a look. Cashmere goats originated from Kashmir in India, and their wool is obtained from a soft, downy undercoat, not the coarse outer hairs we see. But these large beasts with twisted horns are valued for more than their coats. They're used as pack animals, as well, and as a source of milk. And, when shorn of their coat for wraps and hats, each one offers up its own distinctive color.

Black, brown, gray, white, and buff show up on herders watching from a nearby stone hut. They wear clothing to match their charges—one adorable round-faced boy toddles nearby in a brown knitted cashmere hat.

Another stone hut offers tea alongside a low stone wall on which to set down our packs. We take a break in the company of other hikers, most of them local, with bronzed skin and wide-set brown eyes. They carry the traditional cone-shaped woven basket, or *doko*, with a brow strap typical of Nepali porters. Many also carry bundles of 10-foot long wooden sticks, trimmed from a small tree or shrub.

After several minutes of resting at our own wooden table, and they at theirs, I rise to get my jacket from my nearby propped-up pack. Taking a chance at least one of the men speaks English, I turn to their group and ask, "Why do you carry the sticks?"

Drawing only stares and blank looks, I turn back to our table, imploring Amita to translate for me, and she repeats what I said in a language they understand. Their expressions modified, they answer the question for Amita, and she turns back to me. "They are poles to hold up their lodging."

"Oh," I say, forming the shape of an 'A' with my hands. "Teepee!"

To my delight, several of the men nod and smile in response, repeating "teepee" in agreement.

I'd forgotten about the recently discovered kinship between Tibetan natives and some Native American tribes. I'm not sure if "teepee" is the proper term to use, but at least we understand each other, and I now know why they carry the sticks. I also have a greater respect for how much the people here know about ancient cultures around the rest of the world.

Later, as we get up to leave, Adam asks us to stay longer so he has time to fill the water bladder in his pack.

Paul begins to protest, whereupon I interrupt them both by saying, "You might need to have a bit more patience with our son today, Paul. After all, he did manage to save this day for us. Were it not for his persistence, we'd be heading down the mountain instead of enjoying these wonderful views."

"Well, OK, maybe just this once," says Paul with a sheepish grin. "I have to admit that maybe he was right about staying another day. I'd rather be doing this right now than almost anything else I can imagine."

Turning to his son, he says, "Here, let me use this water bottle to pour into your bladder. Refilling it will go much faster that way."

Chapter Twenty-Nine

TEA STOP TO YAK KHARKA

A middle-aged Tibetan man stands before us on a flat narrow ridge leading to Yak Kharka. He has a barely visible mustache and wears a Nike cap with matching navy sweat pants and a short military style jacket. Beside him, on the ground, is a brown wool blanket covered with handmade jewelry and trinkets that he offers for sale. He speaks into a cell phone while I look at his wares. The others move on, but I'm intrigued by this juxtaposition of jewelry salesman, cell phone, and Himalayan backdrop. I select a yak bone necklace with letters that spell "Om mani padme ohm" in Tibetan letters across my neck.

"It means 'good luck'," he says in perfect English, then he presses his palms together to bow his "Namaste."

After I pay him, I bow in return, hoping my new necklace brings with it a special charm for me today.

Minutes later, I gaze to my left where the Jharsang Khola River cuts its way to the bottom of the gorge. It had joined another river, the Khangsa Khola, just above Manang, to form the Marsyangdi. Now we're further up the headwaters, but not so far as to escape its land-altering effects. We must cross the Jharsang Khola River, yet again, and the gorge has only grown deeper. Clasping the necklace at my throat, I gaze across a suspension bridge that stretches more than 600 feet across a seemingly bottomless chasm.

Over my shoulder, I see two porters, each with heavy dokos on their backs following behind us. They're too far away to pass, yet close enough to present a real threat. If they cross the bridge the same time we do, they could create a minor earthquake on the bridge. We measure the distance between them and us, hastening our speed.

Amita steps onto the bridge first, her walking poles held behind her neck, each hand resting beside her shoulders. She strides easily, confident in her balance and the integrity of this suspension bridge. The scene inspires confidence, but leaves me somewhat annoyed at her total lack of fear.

When she and Adam reach the other side, I take my first tentative steps forward, my legs turning to jelly as I move onto the bridge. The porters draw closer, so Paul hangs back, hoping they'll wait their turn, and cross the bridge behind him.

Trying not to grab on, I skim my right hand above the three-foot-tall chicken wire wall, a flimsy banister that repeatedly snags my glove on jagged wires pointing skyward from the top. I'm about a third of the way across when both porters breeze past Paul and step heavily onto the bridge.

"Let them pass," Paul commands from behind my frozen back, but I'm not sure I can. I've never passed anyone on a bridge like this before, so I don't know what to expect. Will the bridge tip to the right if I step aside? I take a tiny step back and stand sideways, as the floor of the bridge begins to bounce. They pass by without so much as a sideways glance, while a silent scream sticks inside my throat. I root myself to the bridge, absorbing every tremor up and down my spine and praying a bigger bounce won't cause my feet to leave the floor. Only when the bridge quiets do I dare to move again.

My pulse still rages in my ears as I reach the other side, but I'm jubilant, having slain yet another beast. Paul comes from behind, holding up his palms to slap his salute. We slap palms, and I slap those of Amita and Adam, once again forgiving each of them their youthful lack of fear.

Turning to Adam, I say, "I think it's time Amita has a nickname. I can't call her 'Budi,' or wife, like you do. I need a name exclusive to me. Tell me— what's the Nepali word for 'daughter-in-law'?"

"Buhari," says Amita, "You can call me 'Buhari' because that means 'daughter-in-law.'"

"Hmm," I say, "That sounds too formal. How about we shorten it to 'Bu', not Boo, spelled 'B-o-o', but Bu, 'B-u', short for Buhari. Would that be all right?"

"That would be fun," she says, and so the matter is settled.

A solid-looking lodge and restaurant complex sits on the near side of the village of Yak Kharka. A low stone wall separates it from the street and delineates a stone patio with courtyards on both sides. Along with fellow trekkers, we stand beside our backpacks, deciding what to do from here. Adam and Amita wander off, telling us they'll investigate our options for lodging. They'll remain true to our agreement not to overspend.

They choose from rows of rooms arranged motel-style behind us, ignoring the more expensive yellow bungalows off to one side. Our rooms, tiny in size, achieve the stated purpose, but no more. We stow our backpacks next to a single bed in each room, and turn around with barely enough room left for us to walk out again.

The toilet room is exceptional for cleanliness, its inside resplendent in white tile, but getting to it involves a five-minute exposure to freezing temperatures most hikers prefer to avoid. In spite of the annoyance, we've made peace with these interruptions to our sleep, referring to them euphemistically as the shedding of "holy water," a process necessary to ensure our bodies acclimatize.

A second-floor room on the north side of the courtyard doubles as both restaurant and lounge. Wide low benches line walls softened by long vertical folds of cloth decorated in red and white flowers. Warm sunlight flows through floor to ceiling windows that give stunning views of tall, jagged peaks stretching across the skyline beyond. Below them sits our dwarfed row of cabins, the peaks so close we could almost reach out our window at night to touch them.

A dozen rectangular tables double as game boards, and stuffed pillows and seat cushions encourage slouching and sitting cross-legged while playing cards or chess, and reading from piles of outdated Western magazines. We spend the remainder of the afternoon relaxing here in the company of other hikers.

At six o'clock, we order our dinner. Amita expects hers to be served in a special room for guides. Since she's the only woman guide, she waits with us for it to be served. First, she's told it isn't ready, then that it's waiting, and, where is she?

Long after we've finished ours, Amita's meal finally arrives. "A mix-up in the kitchen" is the explanation they offer as the reason. She shouldn't have insisted on waiting with us instead of at the all-male table of guides.

Not willing to let the incident slide, Amita finishes her meal with us, then deliberately takes her plate back to the kitchen herself. She identifies the staff responsible for the "mix-up," then tells them they've behaved badly because of her gender. "There's no excuse for your rude behavior." she says, "and if it continues, I will let my family and friends in Pokhara know what you've done."

What may seem like an idle threat to a foreigner, carries real weight in Nepal. Caste and family connections do matter, and the people who work in the kitchen here may be seasonal, spending the rest of their time working in Amita's home town. Misdeeds have a way of catching up.

Still inwardly seething, Amita returns from the

kitchen and nestles quietly beside Adam. Her telling of the story, still fresh on her mind, leaves me wanting to shrink away from this uncomfortable scene. But to do so, would negate the discomfort Amita has already endured in the botched service of her meal. Adam sees nothing wrong with her taking the restaurant staff to task. He offers comfort and encouragement to soothe and calm her.

I'm tempted to feel sorry for Amita, born into a culture where women have virtually no rights. But, suppression of civil liberties only works well where no opposition exists. Amita knows how to stand up for herself, making her spirit a difficult one to break. Warming to her courage, I silently admit my own courage has often failed me when confrontation would have been the wiser course.

After dinner, a dusting of snow covers the patio as we cross it to get to our rooms. Trying not to think about the ramifications deep snow would bring to any upward climb, we fall into our beds. Thin quilts mean we'll need our sleeping bags as an extra layer tonight. Sleep is intermittent but restful for Paul and me, despite two trips we take outside in the middle of night.

As my body goes through the process of acclimatization, I feel my mind making adjustments as well. I'm learning to accept the differences between me and my new daughter-in-law, and learning to think more broadly than the society into which I was born. If I can grow and mature at my age, then the barriers I've felt between Amita's culture and mine must surely be less than I'd feared.

We're forming a bond, glued by our shared experience here and the knowledge that, for as long as this journey lasts, neither of us wants the other to fail.

Chapter Thirty

YAK KHARKA TO THORUNG PHEDI

As we leave Yak Kharka, black forms dot the hillside opposite, then gradually come into view. The creatures from which the town gets its name calmly graze both sides of the trail, claiming it as their domain, and making us feel like intruders. Large and shaggy, they resemble cows with wide-spaced horns, but with faces longer and more triangular. They don't moo so much as snort and growl, like the revving of a motorcycle engine: "va-room, va-room."

This day, as we skirt around the north face of Gangapurna we hug the dry valleys and troughs. Six-hundred feet of elevation gain and another long suspension bridge stand between us and the nearest safe drinking water station at Ledar. The top of the cloud-shrouded 24,000-foot peak forms a wall of white to our south, and seems to follow us, as it has every day since we left Manang.

Purified with Adam's chlorine tablets early this morning, the water we drink is sufficient to sustain us, but leaves us looking forward to other liquids without the chemical after-taste.

We find plenty of drinking water inside one of a group of flat-roofed stone huts arranged on either side of the trail. In addition, we see temporary shelters erected among them, some of which may have been built by the same Nepali hikers we met at that teahouse far below. Each of the shelters owes its support to ten-foot long wooden poles, but unlike the classic cone-shaped Native American teepees, these shelters are low and rounded, somewhat like a dome. Large squares of fabric stretch tightly over three or four arched poles which are fastened to them on both ends. Ropes and cords tie them securely to the ground.

The campers have chosen their spot wisely, since the ground here is both relatively wide and flat, and even the toilet buildings offer an excellent view. Gangapurna forms a triangular wall of white which dominates the skyline to the south, and resident yaks make precious milk possible for our tea.

We discover the real reason they camp here when we look high above us on the mountainside. People cluster and mill about so far away we are barely able to see them. Incredulous, we study their movements, wondering what they can possibly be doing up there.

"They're probably gathering *yarchagumba.*" says Adam. "It's a fungus that lives on caterpillar larvae, killing, and turning it into a mummy, until a little stalk-like fruiting body emerges from the corpse."

"Fascinating," I say, peering up at them. "But why are they looking for it here?"

"It only grows at these altitudes, and mostly in

the Himalayas. It's worth a lot of money, especially here in Nepal. Just one will pay a typical working man's salary for a day. It's supposed to improve libido."

"It figures," I say, "that and rhino horn. Well, at least they don't have to kill a rhino to get it, but those are some pretty steep mountains they're climbing. There must be dozens of people up there."

"More like hundreds. Nepal has trouble keeping the kids in school at this time of year. Whole families join in the hunt."

After filling every water container we carry, we start walking again, only to see in the distance the next suspension bridge. It stretches across the river gorge like the single strand of a gigantic spider web, with multiple baby spiders crossing it at the same time. As we approach, I can't help gasping at its size, stretching as it does farther across the river gorge than any of the previous bridges we've encountered. It hangs nearly 200 feet above the barely visible water below.

Clusters of yarchagumba gatherers travel along a distant slope, then break off to move down together, toward the bridge. As many as five or six cross the bridge at a time, making a safe and stress-free crossing for me an unlikely event.

Adam and Amita show no concern about the crossing. Instead, they approach two women standing at the near end of the bridge to ask them about their success with the hunt. They hold up a corpse by its stalk so we can all have a look. Only a few inches long, the shriveled appearance of the caterpillar larvae defies logic as to its value and the lengths to which people go to retrieve it.

Who am I to judge their motives when I've trudged this far into the Himalayas with no known purpose in mind. Isn't their hunt more clearly defined? They gather caterpillar larvae for sale or trade. I simply walk to complete a well-known trekking loop, but completing that loop means I must go over a very high pass, and now this very long suspension bridge.

Still questioning my motives and whether I can do it, I will my feet to keep moving, determined to get this over as soon as possible, before I can think about what I am doing, and before more caterpillar hunters step onto the bridge.

Locking into step behind Bu, I hope she'll somehow help me to get across. I'm not as rattled as before, having built my confidence from a succession of prior bridges, but I still struggle to maintain focus, to stay in a mind-numbing trance. *"The ants go marching one by one, hurrah, hurrah..."* The lyrics emerge from a childhood memory, sustaining a drumbeat in my head. They help me keep close behind my daughter-in-law.

> *"The ants go marching seven by seven*
> *The little one stops to pray to heaven*
> *and we all go marching down, and around,*
> *to the ground to get out of the rain,*
> *boom, boom, boom..."*[1]

---

[1] "When Johnny Comes Marching Home" was written by Louis Lambert in 1863. The children's song "The Ants Go Marching One By One" re-used the tune and refrain. Wikipedia 2016.

Ultimately, the song carries me all the way to the other side.

"Wow, I can't believe I made it," I say, hugging Bu.

"That's the last bridge before the pass," Adam tells me, "and the longest ones are behind you now."

Looking back at the bridge, I breathe an audible sigh of relief, shaking my head in disbelief. *I summoned the courage, and used tricks to numb my mind and keep my feet moving across it.*

So many other foreign travelers, most of them younger and braver than I am, will cross this bridge and think nothing of it, but for me it was something else. It was a huge challenge.

The caterpillar gatherers around us won't be impressed by what I've done. They've known a time when there wasn't a bridge, or only a rickety unstable one, yet they managed to get around in these mountains just the same. These newer steel bridges were built for tourists. Crossing them doesn't count as a great accomplishment for many Nepalis. No, I'll have to keep what I did to myself, shared only with these witnesses by my side.

The third teahouse we visit today waits just beyond the bridge. Displayed on a table out front are candy bars and apples. Paul and I buy one of each, while Amita speaks with the woman who runs the teashop. I listen while the woman tells her as many as 1,300 caterpillar hunters roam the mountains today.

"You should be careful," Amita translates, "as you cross the slope ahead, because it's prone to landslides. Just one rock loosened from above can send you tumbling into the gorge."

Our gaze fixes on the river valley ahead, the left side completely covered in shale. A thin trail offers only single-file traffic through it until it wraps around the bend and continues on out of our sight.

Amita confidently takes the lead, and Adam follows closely behind. I walk after them, with eyes to the front, placing my feet carefully on the shale, but with frequent scans of the high slope to my left for anyone walking above. Looking back, Paul walks behind me, and in front are my two dear ones. Despite our successes together, a sense of foreboding consumes me.

"Please tell Amita to be careful, Adam," I say. "This may be the most dangerous part we've crossed yet."

We've always been careful, but that isn't always enough. Even experienced hikers can die from a simple fall when a head hits a rock. For us to think we're immune from misfortune isn't wise or realistic for any of us today.

In each of the activities we enjoyed together while our son was growing up, some risk always played a part. For instance, on a river rafting adventure, our 12-year-old Adam fell over the side and found himself stuck underneath the raft.

"Mom, I just walked out, like they told me to," he said, when we pulled him up and over the side to get him back into the raft.

I smiled and hugged him, concealing the terror I'd felt only a moment before, when my whole world had gone dark.

Linda Schuyler Horning

Chapter Thirty-One

THORUNG PHEDI

Thorung Phedi materializes with our band of hikers still intact. The 6-foot-wide covered gate provides a nice photo op, while three signs written in English advertise the lodge and restaurant, as though competition for business here were as strong as anywhere down below. The complex of buildings, also known as Thorung Base Camp, is bordered on two sides by vertical rock walls. Just before it and to the left, a steeply slanted dirt trail with switchbacks leads up toward the pass.

That journey we'll save for tomorrow, though small groups of climbers behind us have already chosen to trudge up that route, the only one leading out from here. They'll sleep tonight at High Camp, 1000 feet higher than Thorung Phedi. We will sleep low and climb high, gaining our last 3,000 feet tomorrow in a single day, but we'll be reducing the chance of suffering altitude sickness before we start our descent on the other side. Though our climb tomorrow will be longer, we're hoping our luck of the last two days will continue to hold out.

The accommodations here are superior to anything we would have found at High Camp. In fact, I am amazed at how much Thorung Phedi has to offer, given the fact it has no access to any navigable roads. Guest rooms surround a large stone courtyard, behind which two concentric circles of lodgings rise up the hillside beyond. Each lodge admits sunlight through large multi-paned windows of glass, and many have their own bathrooms, a significant advantage to travelers staying here where cold nighttime temperatures prevail.

It seems prudent that we hire a porter today to carry our heavier baggage over the top, but we don't know whether we'll find one on short notice and in such a remote location as this. Adam and Amita, anxious to settle the issue, set out on a mission to find one soon after we arrive. Amita will bargain in Nepali, while Adam represents the Western tourist dollar. We hope there are porters here ready to serve.

"Good luck, you two," Paul shouts after them. "We're counting on a good strong back to get us over that pass."

Meanwhile, in the restaurant on the opposite side of the courtyard, another glass window reveals a stunning view of the sheer rock wall behind us, rising out of a dry rock-filled gorge. Aromas of fresh-baked bread, along with Mexican and Asian spices fill our nostrils as Paul and I step inside.

The large rectangular space is filled with hikers, most still covered in their stocking hats, but now their faces look familiar, since we've seen them before on the trail. We wave hello as we enter, and several wave their hellos back to us.

Paul and I occupy one end of a 10-foot table near the front of the room; we share the other end of the table with multiple cell phones, waiting their turn to be charged. Adam and Amita join us soon after, offering their ready thumbs-up as the answer to our silent prayer.

Pulling out his deck of playing cards, Adam is ready to deal our first game of Texas Hold 'em, when a young French woman named Camille asks if she and Jasper can join in.

We jump at the chance, recognizing the opportunity as one for getting to know them more than as just a familiar face. We play several hands, order our meals after the first two, and then continue to play long after it's served. A hand I win after bluffing my son draws peals of laughter from everyone at the table, and a good-natured thumbs-up from Adam and his dad.

Impulsively, I jump up to grab my cell phone off its charger and take it to the front of the room. Handing it to the British co-owner at the counter, I ask her to get as many people in the picture as she can.

"Heads-up, everybody!" I say, and waves and shouts echo to the back of the room.

As I retrieve my camera, I thank my young accomplice and offer my compliments on her surprising selection of food.

"It's beyond what I could have imagined," I say, "given this elevation and its relative isolation from motorized transportation in Nepal. How do you get your supplies?"

"They come over the pass," she responds, as if it's a walk in the park.

Dressed in a hiking shirt and Pashmini scarf, she peers up at me from behind her laptop, fully embodying the Himalayan adventure-seeker she is.

"But how?" I ask, sweeping my hand by the large window. "What do you do if one of these windows should break?"

"It comes on the backs of porters, of course," she says, and as an afterthought, "sometimes they use mules."

That flippant can-do attitude, as well as the impressive strength it requires, is what continues to humble me in this world where ordinary is never enough. Who here cares if I crossed that last bridge, or climbed more than 1,600 feet higher today? Everyone here did it as well, and many probably climbed another 1,000 feet to High Camp, just because they could.

On the other hand, I feel a bond here despite the difference in our ages. It's what compelled the others to shout their hellos and for Camille and Jasper to ask if they could join us. Paul and I have earned the respect we crave in our senior years. We won't always be able to climb mountains, but just by being here now, we've proved we're capable of doing something special today.

Tomorrow will be the real test, and those who still have more to prove will start out early and fast, hoping they'll be the ones to get over the pass first.

We retire early to our rooms to sort through our belongings. I will carry only a camel pack full of water and some extra layers I'll need to stay warm. Paul will wear my pack, emptied of its contents and much of its extra weight. Adam and Amita will carry more, but since they hired a Nepali man, about 30 years old and strongly built, our extra gear will make it to the top on his back.

I'm left to sleep in the long underwear I'll wear under my clothing tomorrow. The extra layers feel warm and toasty as I climb into our frosty bed. Paul's medically aided sleep comes easily, while I find it much harder to give in. Fear and gratitude occupy my consciousness, each vying for first place, until I realize this is nothing new in my life at all.

Fear of losing family, gratitude for lives well lived —these two provide the framework for an existence which often separates us from the people we hold most dear. Going forward, times like this will be memories to share, but right now I'm left with this question: *"How will I temper my fear of loss with my gratitude for how much we've been able to grow?"* I will seek balance, and breathe.

Chapter Thirty-Two

THORUNG PHEDI TO THORONG LA

Harp music plays from my cell phone at 4 a.m. Turning it off pitches us back into total darkness. Staggering toward the wall, I reach for the switch to turn it on. Muffled voices already come from outside.

"Wake me up when it's over," groans Paul from the bed.

"Not a chance," I say. "Come on. The others will be waiting."

Dressing quickly, we put on the outer layers we laid out the night before. Everything else has been given to our porter who bound it up in a big round yellow bundle. We step outside just in time to see him settling under its weight, Adam's big backpack lashed to the underside.

The entire load is attached to our porter's head-strap, or *namlo,* instead of the wide hip belt we prefer to use. We defer to his expertise in carrying heavy loads, since Nepali porters are known for carrying nearly twice their body weight in this way. They are considered to be the most efficient transport system found anywhere in the world.

Light shines on distant peaks as we begin our

ascent, the air clear and still. Biting cold negates any warmth we can generate through exertion while climbing up the trail. After only 20 minutes, my fingers begin to throb, forcing me to stop to unstrap my pack and dig out an extra pair of gloves.

Sitting on a convenient boulder, I pull a second pair of gloves over the ones I already wear, breathing deeply, and looking up for the first time. Now I can fully appreciate our four-footed travel companions casually munching the scarce vegetation around us.

It's a herd of about a dozen bighorn sheep, sure-footed and apparently well-adapted to their mountain domain. They seem unaffected by our presence. Noble and statuesque, they walk among us displaying large backward curving rounded horns, a major tourist attraction at 15,000 feet.

We climb the first 1,000 feet inside an hour, finding High Camp the perfect place to rest and check on our condition. The restaurant, dark and full of tables and benches, is deserted except for us; they serve the familiar hot lemon and provide a warm place to rest before we push on.

As my hands begin to thaw, the thumb of my right hand throbs even more than it did before. I discover I've pushed it through a hole in the palm of my glove in my haste to put on a second pair. Rubbing vigorously and blowing hot breath on it helps get my circulation flowing again. At Paul's suggestion, I leave here with a thick pair of wool socks over my gloves as an added guard against frostbite.

We find the path above High Camp bordered by a

snowbank, now several days old. Stepping in the boot impressions of other hikers avoids slippery ice forming on the slope, but while I focus on the snow as a hazard, it presents something else for Amita.

Filled with child-like delight, she runs enthusiastically toward a pile of undisturbed snow, scooping it up to form a snowball, then playfully lofts it toward Adam. Stunned and delighted, the rest of us realize she's never been close enough to reach out and touch snow before.

I love this part of Amita—so much innocence residing in the body of one so mature. While others emerge from lives offering choice and opportunity, she's been held back for many years. Now she's playing catch-up, with the same naive excitement of Western women half her age.

Much as we wish we could stop and play with Amita, our energy is needed for the climb. Slow and steady, with frequent pauses to breathe, over 1,500 feet still wait to be conquered before we reach the top.

Looking back, High Camp is revealed as a small complex of flat-topped buildings blending into a dry landscape. In front of us, mountain peaks shine brilliantly white as day breaks before our eyes. Has the sun actually risen, or is it we who are climbing into the sky?

Our porter rests his pack on a stone ledge while still standing, his body in almost vertical repose. Amita calls him Ram, and tosses friendly comments as we go trudging by.

"Ram, are you resting so soon?" she teases, then later begs him to slow down.

Despite frequent rest stops, Ram has no trouble keeping up with our snail-like pace. No doubt, he thinks us weak and foolish to climb a mountain in this way, but it's this weakness in others that pays a living wage. He could climb this mountain three times faster and probably does it nearly every day.

Jagged gray peaks of stone mix with mounds formed of smooth sand, while other peaks rise above them. Those are completely covered by a cap of snow. So far, we've been lucky. Most of our path is firm and dry, but snow smears the landscape around us, threatening to stand in our way. Blue skies above promise a brighter day.

A modest stone hut sits in a hollow just before the trail winds up sharply again, toward a decidedly steeper climb. It's attended by a man with a face so weather-worn I can't determine his age. He offers us a beverage and candy, smiling through a friendly but toothless grin.

Hot food is absent here, as it would cook too slowly, but the water he boils does so faster and at a lower temperature than it would far down below. Setting down our packs, we enjoy his hot lemon along with some yak cheese and trail bars we brought along.

Having solved our hydration issues, we're presented with yet another task. Outhouses sitting on ground that's permanently frozen have no hole or drop. Rather than add to a distasteful pile of human waste growing inside the outhouse, we take turns finding a new place to wet the ground outside. Privacy in this wide-open landscape exists only when other hikers turn their backs. Due to our slow pace, no other hikers exist within our sight.

At the top of the next rise, we spot a Czech woman we remember from Manang. Alena rests on an outcropping of rock, apparently by herself. She never found her friend, Adrian, whose picture she showed us on her cell phone, nor did she hire a guide. Fiftyish and moderately overweight, she's tells us she's having problems with her legs. Alena talks animatedly with us, then takes our picture, pretending a total lack of worry for the dangerous predicament she finds herself in.

"Continue on without me," she says, "I'll be fine." But her slow movement betrays her, movement we know can't possibly be sustained.

A feeling of guilt sits on each of us as we move on, sadly saying our goodbyes. Turning to Amita, I ask her to talk with Ram about whether there will be others coming after us who might help.

"Yes, there will be porters, and they'll come from both directions for several more hours after us." But, in his voice I hear a note of irritation.

I realize the services Ram offers are the same ones Alena decided to avoid. By taking this trail alone, she puts not only herself in danger, but risks the lives of porters like himself who might be called upon to aid in her rescue.

As we walk higher, we see Alena continuing to pull her tired body along. She grows ever smaller behind us until at last she disappears from our view.

The terrain flattens briefly to reveal a magnificent snow-blown moonscape, bordered on all sides by sparkling mountain peaks. Swept clean after each successive storm, this place leaves only bamboo pole markers hung with wind-torn prayer flags as evidence of other more turbulent days. No large rocks or trees exist to offer shelter from blizzard winds or numbing cold, but we have no need of them today. Stopping to breathe every three or four steps is the only price we pay for this privilege of walking on top of the world.

Adam asks me for my cell phone to film a panorama of the scene. He starts by announcing where we are and who he is filming, catching me in a close-up, then Paul, standing far off while leaning on his hiking poles and catching his breath. Bu appears in the last few seconds, jumping up and waving happily—our smiling elf.

Such distractions relieve the monotony of climbing, but fail to move us further along. The pass continues to elude us through several more long and arduous hours. With each hard-won step, we learn the limits of individual endurance, gradually answering the question for ourselves how much effort it will take to rise above 17,000 feet.

As I walk, the reason I do this begins to gel in my mind. My life, at 65, has become a series of tests of my physical performance. By no means a competitive athlete, I fight each day to keep myself well, a respectable achievement in the face of inevitable decline. My coaches are these two men with me, challenging me at every turn, and while sometimes I balk, I end up forging ahead, reaching new heights I never thought possible before.

The pass materializes in front of us when it's nearly 11:00 a.m., but no audience precedes us, no leader strikes up the band. We are alone, except for the teahouse attendant, who dutifully offers a drink. The cost is expensive, nearly twice the rupees we normally pay, but we order hot lemon anyway, seeing it as the only way to celebrate our success.

Clinking cups with each other, and with Ram, we see him already unfastening his burden. Having completed his task for the day, he empties the contents of his bundle into a neat pile for us to sort through.

Ram bows to us his best namaste, and we bow in return, sincere in our appreciation. We want him to know how much his effort has meant to us.

A grin lights up Ram's face, and with nothing more to carry, he nimbly skips back in the direction from which we came. He'll be back in Thorung Phedi before we're halfway finished with our hike down the other side.

Namaste—one word for greeting, the same for gratitude. A single word that tells a Hindi we see him as divine.

Chapter Thirty-Three

DESCENT TO ETERNITY

Redistributing what Ram carried for us, we prepare to descend the mountain with new weight on our backs, but first, we must record this monumental event. A sign about 4-feet wide and draped with dozens of prayer flags suffices for exactly that. It reads:

THANK YOU FOR VISITING MANANG
THORUNG-LA PASS[2]
5416 m.
CONGRATULATION FOR THE SUCCESS!!
HOPE YOU ENJOYED THE TREK IN MANANG
SEE YOU AGAIN!!!

The sign serves as a focal point in multiple pictures we take with the four of us assembled on either side, the activity postponing our inevitable journey down the mountainside. A distance remains that is nearly twice as far as the one we have already covered.

As we begin our descent, mule trains and porters pass us from both directions, just as Ram told us

2This spelling is an accurate representation of the sign. Most maps spell Thorong La with an 'o' and no hyphen.

they would. The mules plod onward as if without drivers, fully accepting their lot in this life. Like prayer flags and prayer wheels, they're part of the landscape, a contribution to the character of this wonderful place. Porters run downhill at speeds incomprehensible in this kind of terrain, leaving us speechless with admiration, and hoping none of this part of Nepal will ever change.

The downhill slope takes its toll, turning our bodies into nothing more than sore and tired muscles connected to aching joints, but instead of wishing all this were over, I begin to dread its inevitable end.

Reaching the pass was never the best part, the climax we all waited for. It was just being here together with family, our two generations working together toward a common goal. Here, we were free to give and receive love, and show concern for each other in a way that would have been unlikely anywhere else.

At a rest stop, Paul takes the precaution of applying an Ace bandage to his knee. Amita watches closely, then asks if she can also have one. Without hesitation, Paul reaches into his pack and pulls out a spare. As Adam wraps it tenderly around her leg, Paul and I exchange knowing glances. We know Amita doesn't need an Ace bandage, since she's the youngest and strongest one here, but all three of us jump at the opportunity to show her how much we care.

After more hours of walking, we see a small lodge surrounded by pastures, sitting nestled behind a grove of trees, the first ones on this descent. Seen from far away, it still takes hours for us to approach. Finally reaching it, we step inside. A middle-aged woman, kind-hearted and gentle, offers soup to replenish our fluids and chairs for a needed rest. We linger in the courtyard around a white painted table, our talk limited by the energy it takes to converse.

Far off on a grass-covered hillside, cows run ahead of a fast-walking man who waves his hands in the air. No longer capable of such movement ourselves, we stare at the scene, sharing comments with each other as if watching on an outdoor movie screen.

"I wonder if they grow lop-sided," I say, "from walking downhill like we did today."

"Probably not," responds Paul in a subdued, almost trance-like state, "but I wonder what type of milk they give after shaking their udders that way."

No roads lead from here, so the only way to reach our destination is to start walking again. Muktinath lies still farther down the valley and across another suspension bridge. Daylight holds while we close the distance, but my feet beg for mercy and exhaustion wracks my body. Paul doesn't complain, but a quiet expression of determination speaks volumes about how well he's holding up.

Adam and Amita, suffer far less than Paul and me, and fill with youthful excitement the closer we get to Muktinath. Reaching the temple complex at the edge of town, Amita can no longer contain herself. She runs ahead of us through the open gate, where a pagoda-style temple holds a statue she's been waiting to see.

For Amita and other followers of Vishnu, Sri

Muktinath represents one of eight of the most sacred of Hindu shrines; due to an uncommon arrangement, this site is shared equally with Tibetan Buddhists.

Both philosophies claim that all five elements from which the material universe is made are here: fire, water, sky, earth, and air. Since 1815, fire in the form of a natural gas vent, and water, from the Kali Gandaki River, have made this site sacred for both religions.

At this 12,000-foot elevation, the Annapurna Circuit trail is completed for Paul, Adam, and me. We arrived at this place to end our trek of seven years ago. Joining other pilgrims at the time, we visited the temple much as any tourist would, entering the fire *gompa,* a modest one-story structure festooned with prayer flags and guarded by a Buddhist monk.

A small sign outside the gompa explained the custom of making a wish along with your donation, a suggestion Paul and I were happy to take. We entered reverently, asking humbly for love, happiness, and a sense of purpose for our son. He seemed to us those long seven years ago, to be irresolute and alone.

Paul and I have almost forgotten this prayer in the years that have passed between that time and now, but returning here has brought the memory back to us.

Along the moss-encrusted courtyard wall, freezing cold water flows through each of 108 bull-faced fountain heads, spaced exactly one foot apart. Three of us splashed holy water only on our hands and face during our visit back then, but such a modest dip won't do for our Hindu daughter-in-law. She will accept nothing short of full immersion.

Stripping off most of her hiking clothes, she wraps her torso in a polka dot scarf she brought along. The twelve-hour day of hiking is all but forgotten as she prepares for her ritual bath.

Stepping gingerly at first, she wets her back from the first spout, shrieking from the first bite of cold. Then gathering courage, Amita leaps from spout to spout, laughing, and splashing along the concrete drainage until she claims all 108 spouts.

I stand beside Adam, clapping and enjoying the show. Then glancing sideways, I see in his expression an undeniable truth. Amita is the answer to our long-ago prayer. She's the source of his happiness, his new-found focus in life, and his love. Amita is beyond what any of us could have imagined. It's as if we had to come all the way back here to see what it was we had asked for.

While Adam helps Amita towel off and put on warm clothes, Paul and I excuse ourselves, seeing no need to hide the complete exhaustion we feel. Following the same flat stone pathway as we did that first time, we walk through the wide brick gate with a tile roof that marks the main entry to this site. Together we amble on down the stone staircase that leads to the end of our journey.

Except, I no longer feel like it's the end of a

journey, but the beginning of a new one, and I share those thoughts with Paul.

"She's exactly what we asked for," I say. "Amita makes Adam happier than anyone else could. Lord knows, he tried hard to deny it, but he's deeply in love with her, and might never have felt this way with anyone else."

"Amita is perfect for Adam, when you think about it," says Paul. "She's strong, caring, and spirited—just the kind of woman our son needs."

We hold hands while we descend into Muktinath, a calm satisfaction occupying both our minds; for nothing binds a couple together more firmly than the knowledge their child has someone to love.

We claim victory at having gone over the pass, at staying strong enough to withstand ten long and challenging days, but the part that matters most to all of us is not what we accomplished, but how and what we gained from our trial. Closer as a family now, we're no longer two separate cultures but one, the world of geography and difference that separated us as far away as the sun.

EPILOGUE

Crossing the Thorung La pass in October is considered to be safe, because stormy weather associated with the June–August monsoon season poses no threat. Ironically, our small contingent crossed over Thorong La unscathed in May of 2014, while that same year, a snowstorm and avalanches struck the pass in October.

The storm arose as a remnant of Cyclone Hudhud that backed up over Annapurna and Dhaulagiri after laying waste to India. A loss of power and internet in the Manang District hampered rescue efforts, as nearly six feet of snow fell in a 12-hour blizzard. The storm and avalanches took the lives of 43 people, including 21 foreign trekkers and mountaineers from India, Israel, Canada, Poland, Japan, China, and Slovakia, along with local Nepalis and mountain guides.

Adam shared news about the blizzard, sending Paul and me articles and commentaries about the rescue efforts. "I don't understand why so many people died." he said "Warnings would have gone out."

The typically clear and cool weather in mid-October caught climbers and their guides off guard. Many were ill-prepared to wait out a storm. White-out conditions separated hikers from each other and prevented them from finding shelter. Those huddling up inside stone tea-houses generally made it, if they could fit inside. Some guides died trying to save foreign hikers.

"I heard that many hikers were warned at Thorung Phedi that a storm might be coming, but they went out anyway" Adam said later. "Those who stayed put made it through."

"They probably had a plane to catch," I responded, remembering the tight time-line our group had shared. "Come to think of it, the man in Kathmandu who rented sleeping bags to us wasn't far off the mark. He told us we should carry them 'if you want to live'; that was good advice."

Predictably, Amita wasn't deterred from returning to the Annapurna Circuit trail under safer conditions. Soon after we left Nepal, she accepted a paid position with a nonprofit as a guide for foreign travelers. But, these tourists weren't satisfied with simply hiking the trail; they wanted to run it instead, and Amita agreed to run with them.

Training in Kathmandu with the Hash House Harriers, Amita became acquainted with Nepali international trail runners, who rewarded her with inspiration. She entered local races, running increasingly longer distances to test her endurance.

During a video conference, Adam told us proudly, "She ran 50K last weekend, and I finished only 35." Her enthusiasm for running earned them new friends and became a major social outlet for them both.

On her first run around Annapurna, Amita texted me from Chame before turning in for the night. I could picture her there with her running companions, laughing with them and looking after all their needs. It pleased me to hear she would be paid for her innate thoughtfulness.

"I'm really tired, but I'm having a wonderful time," she said. "The American woman who is running with me is very nice, and she doesn't run very fast."

"That's wonderful, Amita," I responded. "You are amazing. Take me with you in your heart."

"Always," she said.

I ached to be with her, but knew I would only slow her down. This is her time to test her limits while she's young enough to run.

Funds raised by Amita's nonprofit benefit young disadvantaged girls in Nepal, and so her duties include activities that expose them to positive role models. She helps to arrange hiking trips for the girls, and then goes with them to provide support; even casual walks in Nepal often entail steep climbs over precipitous terrain. While Amita helps the girls, she also gains new insights for herself about how Nepali women can contribute more to society.

Meanwhile, Adam continued working in human rights, perfecting his website while mapping more recent violations and communicating them to local law enforcement. One year after our visit, he found a funding source for his project and handed the operation over to a new administrator. He and Amita were celebrating that on their rooftop deck, along with a one-year wedding anniversary meal, when the worst natural disaster in nearly a century hit Nepal —the 7.8-magnitude Gorkha earthquake.

Desperate to hear any word from Nepal, our efforts were stymied by the lack of an internet connection; an electrical storm had occurred near our home in California the night before. Connections in Kathmandu were restored before ours were, enabling relatives to relay information from Pennsylvania, three time zones away. They saw a Facebook posting that revealed Adam and Amita were safe.

While housed in a temporary earthquake shelter in Kathmandu, Adam explored ways he could help. Inquiries led him to a cyber-lab setting up to distribute earthquake relief. Since Adam was familiar with the software they used, they soon put his skills to use. Nearly 9,000 people died and another 22,000 were injured in the disaster, keeping Adam busy for several months. Working outside for safety and often without pay, Adam supervised the mapping of earthquake incident reports, helping to coordinate rescue efforts between relief agencies. Of major concern was the need for temporary shelters. In some areas, avalanches and landslides associated with the quakes had wiped out entire villages, and the monsoon season threatened to compound problems already too complex for many people outside Nepal to comprehend.

Adam and Amita returned to their apartment to find relatively little damage from the earthquake.

Speaking to us by video conference about a week after the quake, Amita spoke first.

"The looters didn't find our place while we were away," she said. "Our roof-top water tank was leaking, but I fixed it before Adam came home. Now we can take hot showers again. Also, a lot of things fell to the floor, but only a few dishes broke."

"It's hard to relax when we have so many aftershocks," said Adam. "They happen almost every day."

One aftershock that occurred on May 12 was nearly as strong as the original earthquake, and to make matters worse, Nepal's new constitution was finalized amid the turmoil, creating an intense political reaction. Two main ethnic groups in the Terai region demanded greater representation in Parliament and a re-drawing of provincial boundaries. Strikes, blockades, and protests stalled an already battered economy, hampering the import of petroleum supplies, medicines, and relief materials. The price of basic necessities skyrocketed while schools and factories closed their doors. Restaurants turned to wood for fuel, worsening air pollution and threatening additional deforestation.

Adam visited us in California for Christmas that same year. Amita couldn't travel with him, because she didn't have a visa. Gathering around the Christmas tree, we plugged in our laptop nearby. Amita waved to us from the other side of the world.

One by one, we opened our presents in front of the laptop, so Amita could see. It wasn't the same without her being here, but we made the best of what we could not change.

"I'm so glad you liked the slippers," she said. "I knitted them myself, and the necklace was really fun to make."

The next year, Paul and I traveled in Nepal during Tihar, Nepal's Festival of Lights. We visited family in Pokhara, then brought Amita's mother with us on a safari in Chitwan National Park. We rode elephants, viewed rhinos and crocodiles, and shared many delicious meals. None of it would have been possible without our special connection to Nepal.

We will continue to visit Nepal as long as we are able, and Adam will visit us. One day Amita may come along. Beyond that, I cannot say. Whatever Adam and Amita decide to do with their lives is beyond our control, but we will be with them, or behind them, as long as we can. Many obstacles remain, but opportunities continue to open. We've already received the greatest gift any family could want, simply because we learned to embrace change as it came into our lives.

GLOSSARY

achar – A pickled article of food popular among Asians.

Agni – Hindu god of fire.

aloo dum – Aloo is a South Asian term for potatoes. This is a Nepali dish of spicy potatoes.

altitude sickness – The effects (as headache, nausea, or swelling of the brain) of oxygen deficiency in the blood and tissues developed at high altitudes having reduced atmospheric pressure.

Bindyabasini Temple Complex – The famous collection of Hindu temples located on a hilltop in Pokhara.

budi – Nepali for wife.

buff – Meat from domestic Asian water buffalo originating in South Asia.

buhari – Daughter-in-law in Nepali.

dal bhat – A traditional meal of the Indian subcontinent, popular in many areas of Nepal.

dhup – An extruded incense; sandalwood.

doko – A basket, hand-woven into a conical shape, used by porters to carry goods.

dudh chia – Milk tea in Nepali.

Durga – Goddess of War, Victory of Good over Evil, The Invincible One, Fierce form of Mother Goddess.

expat – Short form of expatriate; a person who resides in a country other than that of their citizenship.

Ganesha, Lord Ganesha – Represents the Supreme Being, capable of removing obstacles and ensuring success in all human endeavors.

gompa – A term used in Tibetan regions to refer to a variety of religious buildings.

Gorkha earthquake – The April 2015 Nepal earthquake that killed nearly 9,000 people and injured nearly 22,000 people.

Hash House Harriers – An international group of non-competitive running social clubs.

hookah – A single- or multi-stemmed instrument for vaporizing and smoking flavored tobacco.

Kali Gandaki River Gorge – The Gandaki River is one of the major rivers of Nepal, and a left bank tributary of the Ganges River in India.

keffiyeh – An Arab headdress consisting of a square of cloth folded to form a triangle.

khata – A traditional ceremonial scarf common in cultures where Tibetan Buddhism is practiced.

kurta – A tunic or dress with loose pajama pants or tights worn underneath.

mani wall – Structure of intricately carved stone tablets with the inscription "Om Mani Padme Hum."

Marsyangdi River – A river which starts from a confluence of two mountain rivers—the Khangsar Khola and the Jharsang Khola, located northwest of the Annapurna massif at an altitude of 11,811 feet (3,600 meters) near Manang village. Alternate spellings are Marshyangdi or Marysyangdi.

masala – The Hindi word for spice.

masala omelette – A spicy omelette popular in Nepal and India.

Namaste – In Hinduism this means "I bow to the divine in you."

namlo – A forehead strap used together with a doko basket by Nepali porters for transporting goods

Om Mani Padme Hum – The first word Om is a sacred syllable found in Indian religions. The word Mani means "jewel" or "bead," Padme is the "lotus flower" (the Buddhist sacred flower), and Hum represents the spirit of enlightenment.

paneer – A fresh cheese common in South Asia.

Paungda Danda – A mountain notable for its western rock face that dramatically rises 4,900 feet (1,500 meters) above the Marsyangdi River.

Rastafari – A follower of the religious and political movement begun in Jamaica in the 1930s.

rupee – The official currency of Nepal. At this writing, 100 rupees roughly equals one American dollar.

saag – A leaf-based dish of greens eaten in the Indian subcontinent.

Sarankot – A 5,250-foot (1,600-meter) mountain west of Pokhara known for its stunning Himalayan views.

sari – A garment, worn by women, that consists of a drape of cloth varying from five to nine yards in length.

sel roti – A Nepali traditional, home-made, sweet, ring-shaped rice bread/doughnut.

sindoor – A traditional vermilion red cosmetic powder worn by married women at the part of their hair.

squat-john – An Eastern-style toilet used by squatting, rather than sitting.

Sri Muktinath – A sacred place located at 12,172 feet (3,710 meters) elevation at the foot of the Thorong La mountain pass.

stupa – A dome-shaped structure erected as a Buddhist shrine.

The Hash – A weekly running event organized by expats.

Tihar, Nepal's Festival of Lights – Tihar is the second-biggest Nepali festival after Dashain. It is considered to be of great importance as it shows reverence to not just the humans and the gods, but also to the animals like crows, cows, and dogs that maintain an intimate relationship with humans.

tikka – A red powder used in Nepal; it is applied to the forehead for spiritual reasons.

timmur – Szechwan pepper, a popular condiment in Nepal.

Treadle Sewing Machine – A sewing machine that is mechanically powered; the operator pushes a foot pedal back and forth—no electricity is needed.

topi – A traditional Nepali cloth cap.

World Peace Pagoda – A Buddhist pagoda-style monument atop 3,609-foot (1,100 meter) Ananda Hill above Pokhara.

yarchagumba – A fungus that grows on insects found in mountainous regions of Nepal and Tibet.

ABOUT THE AUTHOR

Linda Horning is a retired dietitian and diabetes educator. Her experience includes a wide variety of nutrition-related jobs, both in clinical and community settings. She co-wrote <u>The Complete Idiot's Guide to Fasting</u> with Eve Adamson and contributed to <u>Beef Busters</u>, by Marissa Cloutier, M.S., R.D.

Linda's love of writing extends back to her early years on a rural Pennsylvania farm, but now she writes about adventures she shares with her family in the foothills and mountains of the Sierra and on trips overseas. Nepal remains a frequent destination.

Linda has been active with Sierra Writers, having produced their newsletter for several years. Contact her on her Sasu Aama (mother-in-law) website/blog at lindahorning.me or email her directly at lindahorning dot me@gmail.com.

51687838R00150

Made in the USA
San Bernardino, CA
30 July 2017